Empowered to Pastor

Video-based Learning for
Small Group Based Churches

Joel Comiskey

I0142436

JOEL COMISKEY
GROUP RESOURCING THE WORLDWIDE CELL CHURCH

Published by CCS Publishing
6411 Los Arcos Street
Long Beach, CA 90815 USA
1-888-511-9995

Copyright © 2025 by Joel Comiskey. All rights reserved. No part of this publication may be reproduced, stored in a retrieval system, or transmitted, in any form or by any means, electronic, mechanical, photocopying, recording, or otherwise, without the prior written permission of the publisher. Printed in the United States of America.

Cover design by Jason Klanderud

All Scripture quotations, unless otherwise indicated, are taken from the Holy Bible, New International Version®, NIV®. Copyright ©1973, 1978, 1984, 2011 by Biblica, Inc.™ Used by permission of Zondervan. All rights reserved worldwide. www.zondervan.comThe "NIV" and "New International Version" are trademarks registered in the United States Patent and Trademark Office by Biblica, Inc.™

Scripture quotations marked MSG are taken from THE MESSAGE, copyright © 1993, 2002, 2018 by Eugene H. Peterson. Used by permission of NavPress. All rights reserved. Represented by Tyndale House Publishers, a Division of Tyndale House Ministries.

Scripture quotations marked (ESV) are from The ESV® Bible (The Holy Bible, English Standard Version®), copyright © 2001 by Crossway, a publishing ministry of Good News Publishers. Used by permission. All rights reserved.

ISBN: 978-1-950069-61-3

CCS Publishing is the book-publishing division of JCG Resources, a resource and coaching ministry dedicated to equipping leaders for cell-based ministry.

Find us on the World Wide Web at www.jcgresources.com

CONTENTS

CHAPTER I

Biblical Foundation for Cell Ministry: Trinity, Family, and Biblical Context

WATCH THIS VIDEO ▶

https://youtu.be/N-RjXeMib48

S tart with the why. What is the *why* of small group ministry? Many pastors begin their small group journey with grand vision of church growth. They want to be as large as *Yoido Full Gospel Church* in South Korea or the *Elim Church* in San Salvador, El Salvador.

And yes, God wants his church to grow. But God gives the growth in his timing. When the growth doesn't come as fast as desired, many pastors forsake the cell church vision for another hot program on the market.

For a long time, I thought that church growth was the main reason for doing cell church ministry. I obtained my Ph.D. degree at Fuller Seminary and my mentor was Peter Wagner. I wanted to find out how God used small group ministry to grow churches. The doctoral committee commissioned me to study the largest churches in the world.

What an exciting time! I found growth principles common in all these churches and especially how these churches were growing through small groups. I began to write and teach about how small group ministry could bring church growth.

After the Ph.D. I went back to our growing cell church in Quito, Ecuador, which was growing rapidly. Many churches in Quito, however, were also growing rapidly. After 100+ years of missionaries sowing the seed, the harvest had finally come and cells helped reap the harvest.

I was more convinced that if churches could just follow the growth principles I was writing about, they would also grow. I found myself judging slow growing churches, thinking they weren't making the proper adjustments. I would show them.

Then God took me to the backside of the desert, like he had done with his servant Moses. I planted a church in Moreno Valley, California, using the same cell church principles we had used in Ecuador. But the growth was slow. It *seemed* that people preferred to go to a mega church where they could hide among the crowd. Few really wanted to prepare to lead a small group or participate as a team member.

At the same time, I coached pastors in secular countries like Europe and Australia. These pastors also faced challenges. Cell church was not a magical cure and in fact, some members left the church. I struggled. What was the reason for cell ministry?

Slowly God began to show me a better way of doing ministry. I realized that the main reason to become a cell-based church was because it was biblical. Scripture, rather than pragmatism, was the true motivation—the why of small group based ministry.

I began to see Scripture in a new light. While writing my book *Relational Disciple,* my editor, Scott Boren, challenged me to critique North American individualism. I hesitated doing this because I was so thoroughly conditioned with a church growth mentality, which taught that all cultures were amoral and that the goal of the pastor was to find the cultural keys that worked in that particular culture to produce church growth.

Of course, I felt that cell church would produce the most growth, so I tried to tweak cell church to fit particular cultural norms. But it wasn't working. I had to go deeper. In a nutshell, I discovered that *theology breeds methodology.* We first need to establish the biblical foundation and methodology flows from that point.

The Trinity and Community

I realized that God is a Trinity: Father, Son, and Holy Spirit. The Trinity critiques individualism. God is a God of community and in once sense, he is a small group. He loves community.

At that time, I thought that community was a hindrance to church growth. I counseled churches and groups not to become too cozy with each other. Yet, as I wrote *Relational Disciple* I had to come to grips with the over 50 *one-another* passages in Scripture. God, our relational God, desired a loving, caring church. And I had to admit that Scripture critiqued individualism.

I made the break. I returned to constructing my philosophy of ministry from the Bible and not what worked. I gave up my church growth roots that compelled me to promote cell church for the results and planted my flag on biblical truth. But was cell church biblical?

I found out that yes, it was.

Family

God created Adam and Eve to live in harmony to reflect his image. Family in the Old Testament was the foundation of society and the way his chosen people were to glorify him. The nation of Israel was a nation of families.

When I'm doing cell church ministry around the world, I tell pastors and leaders that the first priority is family. I've seen churches multiply rapidly without regard to prioritizing their own families. True success starts at home.

Getting back to the nation of Israel. Yes, they failed to give glory to God. They failed to reflect his image through family.

Christ's method of ministry

When Jesus came, he declared the *kingdom of heaven* has come. Jesus came to establish a new family. And notice that Jesus went into the homes. I counted nineteen times that Jesus entered a home. Jesus knew that unless he could establish his Kingdom where people lived and spent most of their time, his rule would be limited.

Jesus also sent his disciples two-by-two into the homes to declare his rule (Luke 9 & 10; Matthew 10). He told them to find the person of peace and then to stay in the house. The implication was to convert the householder and continue the process through multiplication.

When Pentecost came (Acts 2), the disciples immediately started meeting from house to house and changed the then known world. They were an unstoppable force as they changed society and penetrated the world for Jesus Christ.

All believers could minister and everyone had a prophetic word. The church also came together whenever possible. In acts 2:42-46, we read they came together daily to hear the apostles teaching, while continuing to meet house to house. Paul preached publicly and from house to house (Acts 20:20).

House to House Ministry

The reality is that New Testament ministry was house to house ministry. I don't believe we can truly understand the New Testament without the context of the cell church. We must remember inspiration or inerrancy is the moment when the authors were writing their letters and books that now comprise the Bible. But each of them wrote to a particular context. The New Testament context was house to house ministry.

Paul said to Timothy, "if I am delayed, you will know how people ought to conduct themselves in God's household, which is the church of the living God" (1 Timothy 3:15). Paul is referring here to the house church, God's family, which is the church of the living God. The church met in the home, as we can see from many passages:

- Church in the house of Mary (Acts 12:12)
- Church in the house of Priscilla & Aquila (Romans 16:3-5)
- Church in the house of Aquila & Priscilla (1 Corinthians 16:19)
- Church in the house of Ninfa (Colossians 4:15)
- Church in the house of Archippus (Philemon v.2)

I've written a book called *Biblical Foundations for Cell Ministry*, in which I describe in great detail the biblical foundations for small group ministry.

Reflection Questions

What did you learn from this lesson?

How should our relationship with the Trinity affect our interactions with others?

What should Christ's method of ministry (house-to-house) affect our methodologies today?

Suggested Reading

Books

– *Chapter 2,3,5 of Biblical Foundations for the Cell-Based Church*

Internet articles

Transformed by the Trinity
The Family of God
The House in the New Testament

Download this PowerPoint

Joel Comiskey's PowerPoint on this lesson:

https://tinyurl.com/ympb6vvj

CHAPTER 2

Biblical Foundation For Cell Ministry: Meeting Size and Order, Oikos, Leadership Development, and Celebration

WATCH THIS VIDEO ▶

https://youtu.be/UWkFjC9Z63k

I believe the *why* for small group ministry is the biblical base. God is a Trinity and desires to receive glory through community. The Bible, rather than pragmatic results, should judge everything we do in ministry.

The early church was a house to house ministry and changed the then-known world as a result.

What they did in those house church meetings

Paul said in Colossians 3:16, "Let the word of Christ dwell in you richly as you teach and admonish one another with all wisdom, and as you sing psalms, hymns and spiritual songs with gratitude in your hearts to God." Paul was writing this letter to a Colossian house church. His letter was distributed among the house churches.

Paul exhorts this church to minister to each other through Psalms hymns, and spiritual songs. Paul wanted them to teach and admonish each other through the power of the Holy Spirit.

What else did they do? They ate together and remembered the Lord's death and resurrection. They evangelized, prayed, and shared announcements from around the then-known world. We know the Holy Spirit moved among his gifts which he distributed to each person.

The order of the early church house churches was dynamic and flexible. Everyone participated. I have to remember this when overly promoting a small group order or wanting everyone to follow the same lesson questions. The most important aspect of small group ministry is that people go away built-up and encouraged.

Size of the early house churches

We read in Acts 2 that the upper room could fit 120 people. Was that normative? Actually, that particular home was the exception. Most homes were very small.

I discovered that the size of the early house churches were between 10 and 20 people. You could call them *apartment* churches because most people lived in densely populated cities. Some experts have noted that the city density during the New Testament was greater than cities like Calcutta today. People were packed together. Neighbors could hear the singing and witness the changed lives of their neighbors. The grace of God flowed from one house to another.

Oikos Relationships

The Greek word *oikos* means house. Yet, in the New Testament, the word also had a broader meaning. *Oikos* also meant close relationships like cousins and extended family—those connected to the house.

And it was through these relationships that the early church extended its web of outreach. Family members reached out to cousins, relatives, and close friends.

Oikos outreach today is the best way to win family and friends. People don't care how much we know until they know how much we care. The most effective way to reach out is through need-based ministry.

Developing Ministers from the House Structure

How did they raise up new leaders? Often the host would become the next small group leader. Those enflamed by the Spirit of God would open their homes, invite their oikos, and reach their friends and neighbors. New leaders would then take up the gospel torch.

Leadership in the New Testament was team oriented. Teams of leaders opened up cell groups or supervised existing ones. The New Testament always uses the plurality of leadership.

I go into detail about these concepts in my book *Biblical Foundations for the Cell-based church.*

The connection between house churches

The apostles were the main steering team, followed by the bishops/elders/pastors. All three words were used to describe the same position. Most likely the bishops/elders/pastors coached house churches. Deacons were ministers within the house churches and most likely house church leaders.

The house churches would gather whenever possible to hear godly teaching and receive encouragement. The house churches were not independent entities, but rather were connected through the New Testament leadership structure.

Going back to New Testament Principles

Paul says in Romans 15:14, "I myself am convinced, my brothers, that you yourselves are full of goodness, complete in knowledge and competent to instruct one another." Paul exhorts these Roman believers to remember that the Holy Spirit had made them competent to instruct each other.

Sadly, tradition says the pastor is the one who instructs. In many churches, the subtle message is: "come, sit, sing, listen, give, help some, and come back." The church is Sunday a.m., Wednesday, p.m., in a building. Committees and program support.

But Scripture teaches that people are taught to instruct one another. The Priesthood of all believers learn to do ministry. God's people are the church every day of the week.

Paul says in Ephesians 4:11-12, "It was he who gave some to be apostles, some to be prophets, some to be evangelists, and some to be pastors and teachers, to prepare God's people for works of service, so that the body of Christ may be built up."

Tradition teaches that the pastor is the minister. Pastors lead the church through preaching and caring. Growth is dependent upon the pastor's personal ability. Yet, Scripture teaches that all are ministers and called to do ministry. The role of a Biblical leader is to equip the people for ministry. Growth comes as the people are prepared for ministry

Paul said to Timothy, "And the things you have heard me say in the presence of many witnesses entrust to reliable men who will also be qualified to teach others" (1 Timothy 2:2).

Many pastors think, "If I raise up other leaders, I will not be needed or valued anymore." Yet, Scripture teaches that raising up leaders will help pastors expand the base of ministry. Leaders are always needed to fulfill their equipping ministry role.

Reflection Questions

What did you learn from this lesson?

How does the size of the early house churches apply to your current small groups?

Explain the word *oikos* in your own words. How can you apply this concept in your own small group?

Suggested Reading

Books

- *Chapter 6-9 of Biblical Foundations for the Cell-based Church*
- *Chapter 6 of Reap the Harvest: How a Small Group System Can Grow Your Church*

Internet articles

Developing Leaders from the Early House Churches

How to Define a Disciple

Download this PowerPoint

Joel Comiskey's PowerPoint on this lesson:

https://tinyurl.com/5esuay5y

CHAPTER 3

Making Disciples: The Most Important Biblical Principle

WATCH THIS VIDEO ▶

https://youtu.be/26wOy6LjKlk

Simon Sinek was a successful businessman.. But he was also a bored successful businessman. He knew how to sell things and what he was selling. But he really didn't know why he was selling his products.

He began to study successful leaders worldwide and discovered that they knew why they were doing what they were doing. They had the right motivation behind their leadership. They were passionate about why they were leading.

Many pastors start cell church ministry because they have heard of a famous, growing church doing cell ministry. Maybe they've heard that if they just follow a successful model, they too will experience the same type of growth. The magical success syndrome is common throughout the world today.

Yet, a purer, more biblical motivation must fill the pastor's soul. The best reason to do small group-based ministry is because it's biblical. Yet, saying that it's biblical seems so broad. What is the main biblical base? Or put another way, if there was any one biblical principle deemed the most important, what would that be?

Making Disciples: the Principal Why Behind Small Group Ministry

I believe that *making disciples* is the #1 biblical motivation behind small group ministry. Allow me to explain.

Jesus gave marching orders to his disciples in Matthew 28:18-20: "All authority in heaven and on earth has been given to me. Therefore go and make disciples of all nations, baptizing them in the name of the Father and of the Son and of the Holy Spirit, and teaching them to obey everything I have commanded you. And surely I am with you always, to the very end of the age."

The one command in these verses is to make disciples. And notice that Jesus gave his command to his own disciples, who he had walked with for three years. They asked Jesus questions, saw his miracles, and learned lessons in the group. The group factor was important because they could fail forward, receive corrections, learn from the other disciples, and practice Christ's teaching.

They were becoming like Jesus in the process, and this is what discipleship is all about. Discipleship means to become like Jesus, to be conformed to his image (1 John 3:2-3; Romans 8: 29).

When Jesus told them to make new disciples, he wasn't sending each one off to find one individual disciple. No, he was sending them out to start groups of disciples.

Remember that Jesus had send them two-by-two into the homes (Luke 9-10; Matthew 10). Christ's instructions was to find the person of peace, stay in the home, and allow the home owner to practice hospitality. The broader goal was the multiply the group with new disciples.

We know this because when Pentecost came (Acts 2), they immediately started meeting house to house, just like Jesus had taught them. The early church was a discipleship movement that met house-to-house and celebrated whenever they could (Acts 2:42-46; 5:42; 20:20).

Making disciples is the chief motivation behind small group ministry.

Community

We become like the Trinity as we practice the one-an-others. Our God is one God who exists in three persons. In one sense, he's a small group. Group discipleship is essential because community takes place in the small group context.

Think of Christ's own small group. What a ragtag group of people. Matthew, the tax collector, Peter the fisherman, Judas the rebel, and so forth. They didn't naturally love each other or even like each other. But Jesus washed their feet and then told them to do the same. By the end of Christ's time with them, he could say, "by your love the world will believe" (John 13).

As I do seminars around the world, one question that people often ask is, "I don't get along with *so and so* in my group. What should I do? Should I go to another group?" I like to answer that question by saying, "No, stay there. God will be glorified even more when he gives you supernatural love for that person.

Peter said, "Above all, love each other deeply, because love covers over a multitude of sins" (1 Peter 4:8). Peter was writing to a house church, telling them to cover each other's sins. Peter knew and experienced God's love toward him, even after denying him three times. Peter exhorted the believers to practice that same type of forgiving love.

Someone said that if you want to know if you love someone, just get in a conflict with that person and you'll soon find out how much you love them.

My wife Celyce is a great small group leader. One time she had a lady in her group that incessantly gossiped. Celyce knew she had to talk with this cell member and eventually did. Why? Because Celyce understood she needed to be more like Christ and speaking the truth in love to her was part of that process. She talked to her one-on-one, like Jesus tells us to do in Matthew 18.

Priesthood of All Believers

Another important way we make disciples in the small group is through the priesthood of all believers. Every believer has at least one spiritual gift (1 Peter 4:10) and is an important member of the body of Christ (1 Corinthians 12: 12-26). All of the gift passages were written to house churches.

In the early house churches, each believer ministered and grew to be more like Jesus in the process.

The same is true in small group ministry today. Each person can step out and use their gifts, minister to others, and actively participate. On Sunday, the lay people normally sit and listen. Small group ministry is designed for everyone to be involved.

I've noticed a *secret* in pastoral ministry. The pastor, unlike those who are seated, grows more than the congregation. Why? Because the pastor must trust God when praying for the sick, preparing and delivering the message, counseling those in need, and so forth. Those sitting and listening do very little.

All of this changes in the small group. Everyone is involved, sharing, exercising their gifts, and ministering to others.

I remember when I gave a small group seminar in Connecticut. I had preached that morning and afterwards, those present from Saturday's seminar came together for food and questions. One youth small group leader said, "I prepare really hard for my lesson, but when I lead the group, the youth seemed so bored. What should I do?" The lead pastor and I looked at each other and then we looked at him saying, *Welcome.*

I told the youth small group leader that I had preached that morning and two people were falling asleep, but I had to keep on preaching. I couldn't stop. The pastor said that on Monday, after his Sunday preaching, he remembers all the things he *should have said* in his message. He often feels condemned.

We told this youth leader that he was learning how to be like a pastor. And of course, this applies to the members as well.

Exercising our muscles in small group ministry is critical to become like Jesus and a priest of the living God (Revelation 1:6).

Conclusion

Becoming a disciple of Jesus is much more than small group community or the priesthood of all believers. It also involves evangelism, multiplication, and even participating in the small group system—celebrating together, equipping, and coaching.

We do need to remember that the motivation behind doing small group ministry is to make disciples who make disciples.

Reflection Questions

What did you learn from this lesson?

What does the Bible teach about making disciples?

Why does Joel Comiskey believe that making disciples is the principal motivation for cell-based ministry? What do you believe?

How does community and the priesthood of all believers contribute to becoming like Jesus?

Suggested Reading

Books

- *Chapters 1-4 of Making Disciples in the Cell-based Church*

Internet articles

Making Disciples: the Essence of Small Group Ministry
Discipleship through Community
Discipleship through the Priesthood of All Believers

Download this PowerPoint

Joel Comiskey's PowerPoint on this lesson:

https://tinyurl.com/59f7hptp

CHAPTER 4

Making Disciples: How Evangelism, Multiplication, and the Cell System Make Disciples

WATCH THIS VIDEO ▶

https://youtu.be/NF3Lmw4RvHc

I believe that making disciples who make disciples is the key reason behind doing small group ministry. Jesus gathered his own disciples into a small group, taught them in an interactive environment, allowed them to fail, and then told them to make new disciples (Matthew 28:18-20).

They knew what he was talking about. Jesus had previously sent them into the homes as the main ministry strategy. The disciples followed Christ's strategy when the Spirit came on the day of Pentecost. They immediately penetrated the homes and apartments of the Roman Empire and gathered together whenever possible (Acts 2:42-46; 5:42; 20:20).

As believers exercised their spiritual muscles, invited non-Christians, and loved those *unlike them*, Christianity exploded throughout the Roman empire. The movement was impossible to stop and eventually it became the official religion of the Roman Empire during the days of Constantine.

Evangelism

Evangelism is important in the process of becoming disciples of Jesus Christ. Yes, we know that hell is real and without trusting in Jesus as Lord and Savior, people will go to hell. We have an urgent mission to share the gospel with as many people as possible. Yet, there's also another important ingredient in sharing the good news: we grow as disciples of Christ in the process.

As the group prays, plans, and invites, each member exercises their spiritual muscles and grows to become like Jesus. I believe that every small group needs to intentionally evangelize and reach out to become all Jesus wants them to be.

Let me give you an example. I was supervising one small group and happened to be present as they were planning an outreach activity. The small group leader felt they should do a barbeque to invite and attract unchurched and non-Christian people. One of the small group members resisted that idea saying, "I don't think people will come. We've tried that before. I think we should just concentrate on ourselves." I spoke up saying, "The purpose behind having the barbeque is not primarily how many people show up. Yes, we want that and we'll pray for that end. But the main reason is to become more like Jesus and to exercise our spiritual muscles in the process of reaching out."

I've noticed that many groups don't reach out because of the fear of failure. Yet, the motivation of becoming disciples of Jesus helps us to remember that small group outreach is essential in the process of becoming like Jesus.

Multiplication

A lot of people resist multiplication because they envision small group *division* and tearing apart the group. And some have had negative experiences of saying good-bye to friends and family.

I believe it's important to understand multiplication from the standpoint of making disciples who make disciples. Making disciples of Jesus must be the main focus—not multiplication. Multiplication is the result of making disciples.

I believe the main image of the church in the New Testament is the family of God. Jesus desires to establish new families that reach new communities. My daughter Sarah has been married for 7+ years. I remember when Jake, her husband, approached me to marry Sarah .I could have said, "No, Jake, the only man in Sarah's life is myself." But Sarah wanted to marry and start a new family. Jake, a godly man, loved Sarah and wanted to begin a relationship with her. Now they have three grandboys, and I'm very blessed. But my point is that establishing new families is natural, normal, and part of God's creation process.

The same is true with cell multiplication. Multiplying new families is pleasing to God and desirable. Yet, we cannot multiply unless we have disciples. My definition of a cell group is *Groups of 3-15 people who meet weekly, outside the church building, for the purpose of evangelism, community, and spiritual growth with the goal of making disciples who make disciples that results in group multiplication.* Notice that in this definition I talk about multiplication as the result of making disciples.

I've had to learn this truth the hard way. In the past, I've been so focused on multiplication that I started groups too quickly. I believed I had to multiply after a certain number of months—like six—whether or not disciples were formed. Those groups quickly closed because they lacked prepared leadership. Making disciples who make disciples must be the focus.

And the New Testament talks about sending out leadership teams, so I don't think it's wise to multiply a group until raising up a team of leaders who can continue the process.

Making Disciples in the Cell System

We make disciples in the cell group but also the cell system. We believe the New Testament talks about small groups meeting from house to house and gathering those small groups into larger gathering (Acts 2:42-46).

Celebration gathering

Groups meeting from house to house during the week will gather on the weekend to worship, hear God's Word, and fellowship together.

The larger gathering is a great time to hear anointed, prepared preaching. The small group normally applies that teaching. In the larger gathering, all the groups meet together. In the smaller gatherings, individual groups meet to apply Scripture, evangelize, and grow to become more like Jesus.

The larger gathering highlights the extended family of God. For example, Oscar was part of my small group. When we multiplied the group, I no longer saw Oscar in the cell group, but I did see him on Sunday. Multiplying groups is a lot easier when we know we are not saying a final good-bye.

Pastors can cast the vision for small group ministry, include small group testimonies in the larger group, and shepherd the small group system more effectively. Yet, the overall goal is to make disciples who make disciples.

Coaching Leaders

Coaching each leader is the glue that holds the small group system together. Coaching or supervising is part of the process of making disciples. Small group leaders give to their members, but coaches pour back into the small group leaders through listening, encouragement, care, planning, strategizing, and challenging.

Coaching takes place at larger leadership level and one-on-one between coach and leaders. Some small group churches call their coaches supervisors, but I like the word coach better. Coaching the leaders helps each leaders to remain strong and gives them the resources to continue long-term.

Equipping

Small group based churches ask each member to go through an equipping process that teaches them about Bible basics, how to be set free from besetting sins, how to have a quiet time, how to evangelize, and how to lead a small group.

I believe that anyone in the church can be part of a leadership team that starts a new spiritual family. But the first step is to go through the equipping process. I like to tell churches to decide on only one equipping track with many ways to teach the equipping (e.g. Sunday school, retreat setting, one-on-one, and so forth).

Discipleship equipping gives future leaders the confidence to know what is expected and what to look forward to.

Stay focused on making disciples

Christ's great commission is just as relevant today as it was when he spoke to his disciples. Through the small group and small group system, Jesus prepares disciples who make other disciples. Jesus will build his church, and we have the privilege of participating in what he is doing.

Reflection Questions

What did you learn from this lesson?

How does evangelism and multiplication mold Christians into disciples of Christ?

How does Sunday worship (celebration gatherings) develop Christ-like disciples?

How does equipping and coaching contribute to the process of becoming like Jesus?

Suggested Reading

Books

- Chapters 5-9 of *Making Disciples in the 21st Century Church*

Internet articles

Making Disciples through Evangelism
Making Disciples through Multiplication
Making Disciples through the Larger Gathering
(celebration)
Making Disciples through Coaching

Download this PowerPoint

Joel Comiskey's PowerPoint on this lesson:

https://tinyurl.com/3eekmnzk

CHAPTER 5

Key Principles in
the Cell-based Church

WATCH THIS VIDEO ▶

https://youtu.be/n7llkxnKv3A

Introduction:

As I travel around the world, I often hear about models. One church has had success and then wants everyone to follow exactly what they're doing. Sometimes it's for financial gain or pride. Yet, the problem with following models is twofold: 1. Loss of creativity 2. Division in the church.

When a church follows someone else's model exactly, that church always has to go back to the founder of the model when things don't work out right. In other words, the church loses the creativity to follow God's Spirit and becomes bound to a particular model.

The other problem is the division that models cause. I've seen certain cell church models rip apart churches within denominations. I often can't even mention particular models as I travel around the world because of the terrible division those models have caused.

As I researched small group-based churches around the world, I had to find principles that all of them followed. If one principle was not common in all the cell churches, I had to throw it out.

Three Key Foundations

I tell churches to build on three foundations.

First, the biblical base. We do cell church ministry because we believe it is biblical.

Second, the principles that all cell churches follow.

Third, becoming an example where the church ministers. I believe each church should attempt to implement their own strategy and become an example where they are. As God gives growth, others might want to learn from what God has done through the church. The response is not "Follow my model," but rather, "Follow the principles" and God will give you fruit in your own context.

The first place to look is Scripture. Cell church ministry is biblical. But what about the key principles that growing cell churches follow? Allow me to highlight four.

Dependence on Jesus Christ through prayer.

All of the cell churches in my research were praying churches. Each of them was totally dependent on Jesus Christ to do the work. They weren't depending on their strategies but on Jesus Christ. All these cell churches emphasized prayer and made prayer the base of all they did.

I studied one famous cell church, and they allowed me to stay in an apartment in their church that overlooked the sanctuary. Each morning, I was awakened at 4 a.m. with praise and worship. Then another group came at 5 a.m. and another group at 6 a.m. God answered their prayers and the church experienced a powerful moving of the Holy Spirit.

Now I don't believe we can manipulate God. He is sovereign and we are not. Yet, I believe that God likes to hang out in those churches that pray.

God is the One who blesses churches that pray. I think of Yoido Full Gospel Church in South Korea. They carved out a prayer mountain from a cemetery. 10,000 people pray at that mountain each week.

Other churches have all night or half night prayer meetings. I don't think that there's one way to pray. Some churches have prayer chains, small prayer groups, early morning prayer, late night prayer, and so forth. The main thing is to pray. Whatever works best for your church is the best strategy, but the key is to do it. My wife often says "Joel, when you do these small group based seminars, remember to tell them that prayer is the key."

I have the tendency to veer into the realm of techniques, but God wants me to remember that prayer must be our principal focus.

Senior pastor and leadership team giving strong, visionary leadership

Passionate, committed pastors lead fruitful cell churches. It's not enough for the lead pastor to have the vision-- the vision must have the pastor. I tell lead pastors not to even start their transition until they are sure that this is what they want to do for a lifetime.

Lead pastors will face many cross winds—people trying to pull the pastor away from the cell focus. Unless the lead pastor is passionate and convinced that cell church is biblical and the best way to make disciples who make disciples, it's very easy to stop midstream or go another direction.

I'm always impressed when the lead pastor is regularly attending a cell group or leading one. The pastor's involvement shouts loudly to the congregation that small group ministry is essential. It also helps the pastor to connect the sermon with the cell and to understand what the people are experiencing. Granted, there might be a time when the lead pastor prioritizes coaching and does not lead a cell group, but if at all possible, I think it's important to attend one.

Cell ministry Promoted as the Church's Backbone

I would often hear the phrase "cell ministry is our backbone" as I visited worldwide cell churches. The backbone or vertebrae is central and critical in the human body. My good friend and fellow believer, Kevin Strong, died several years ago of brain cancer.

Yet his *brain cancer* was located in his vertebrae. In other words, the vertebrae is part of the brain.

Small group ministry must not be relegated to "another program." It must be central. What do I practically mean by this? The goal is for all attendees to be part of a small group as the priority. Local churches have other ministries besides cell groups, but in the cell church, the first place to start is cell involvement.

If someone wants to be on the worship team, that person must first be actively involved in a cell group. If they want to be an usher or children's worker, a key requirement is to participate in a cell group. Cells are the backbone, the center of ministry—just like in the New Testament.

Obviously, the process will take time, especially if a church is just starting cell ministry. The fourth principle is about the quality of the small group.

Clear definition of a cell group

Some churches call cell groups everything that is small and a group. This would include Sunday school, prison ministry, ushers, and board membership. But are those small groups cell groups?

I believe it's important to begin with a clear definition. I define small groups this way:

Groups of 3 to 15 that meet weekly outside the church building for the purpose of evangelism, community and spiritual growth with the goal of making disciples who make disciples that results in multiplication

The cell is the church and the church is the cell.

We must not lower the bar of what a cell is.

Once we have a clear definition of what constitutes a cell, then homogeneity (e.g., family, men, women, youth) can flow naturally from that starting point.

I've just highlighted the big four.

Yes, there are other principles, but I go over those other principles in far greater detail in my book *Reap the Harvest.*

Reflection Questions

What did you learn from this lesson?

What principle is the most needful for you at this time?

Describe the prayer life in your church. What can you do to improve it.

As pastor, what can you do to feed the cell vision?

Suggested Reading

Books

- Chapter 3, 7-9 of *Reap the Harvest: How a Small Group System Can Grow Your Church*

Internet articles

The Power of Prayer
Lead Pastor's Role in the Cell Church
Senior Pastor's Growth in Vision (Mario Vega)
Cells Promoted as a the Backbone of Your Church
What is a Cell Group?
What Should You Call Your Groups?

Download this PowerPoint

Joel Comiskey's PowerPoint on this lesson:

https://tinyurl.com/3e568ccr

CHAPTER 6

Three Keys to Pastoral Success

WATCH THIS VIDEO ▶

https://www.youtube.com/
watch?v=gmg7BnIGN80

I've had the privilege of studying cell churches around the world and also coaching pastors in cell group ministry.

I've seen pastors who lead their churches with passion, vision, and clear direction, as well as those who fizzle out and decide that cell church ministry is not worth it. They normally go back to the conventional model saying, "cell church just doesn't work." Or if they stay with it, their churches don't go anywhere.

So what are some of the key principles that I've observed?

First, prayer.

Successful cell church pastors dedicate themselves to prayer first and foremost. Little will happen without the pastor prioritizing his or her own prayer life and a church dedicated to prayer.

God loves to use the cell church strategy but he won't be used by it. I'm always amazed when I visit Yoido Full Gospel Church, the largest church in the history of Christianity. The church grew to 25,000 cell groups, yet, I believe the main reason for such explosive growth is their powerful prayer. 10,000 people pass through prayer mountain each week.

Pastor, what kind of prayer is going on in your church? Are you dedicating yourself to prayer?

Second, start with the why.

Simon Sinek wrote a famous book, *Start with the Why*. In that book, he talks about great leaders who have changed society. He noticed that these leaders knew why they were doing what they were doing. They understood their motivation. They could answer the why question.

Many pastors enter cell church ministry for the wrong reason and they end up fizzling out prematurely. Perhaps they wanted to grow a bigger church. Perhaps they had heard about the tremendous growth in Korea or El Salvador and figured that cell church in itself would make their church grow.

Yet, when the going gets tough and people leave, they end up throwing in the towel and going back to conventional type ministry.

Often the reason for their discouragement and lack of persistence is because they didn't start with the correct *why*. They had false motivations to begin the journey and those false motivations eventually drove them away.

So what is the correct *why*? I believe it's making disciples who make disciples. Jesus gave us one commission, "make disciples of all nations." He started in a small group and those small groups multiplied into new small groups. Yet, more importantly, disciples were formed. My book *Making Disciples in the 21st Century Church* highlights the *why* of cell ministry.

When a pastor understands the *why*, they will persist in the good and bad times.

The third key is harder to understand and even define.

It's what I call development or empowerment. To be fruitful in cell church ministry, a pastor needs to be willing to develop others. They need to readily delegate the ministry. They need to love preparing others to do the work of the ministry through the equipping and coaching. They love to develop team ministry and rejoice when others even preach.

Cell church ministry is all about developing others to do the work of the ministry.

Yet, I see many pastors who love to hear their own voice. They live for the preaching and to have a crowd listening to them. They don't develop a team and need to be present in every meeting. When someone needs counseling, they are normally right there to do it. They lack this key aspect of development.

This is especially hard because a pastor can talk about cell church ministry, attend a cell, and love the vision without being a developer. How are you doing in this area?

Obviously, there are so many more aspects that make or break successful cell ministry. But prayer, making disciples, and developing others are at the heart of cell ministry.

In my book *Leadership Explosion* and *Coach* I talk about developing others through equipping and coaching. This is a great place to start.

Reflection Questions

What did you learn from this lesson?

What is your church doing to promote prayer? What steps can you take to pray more as a church?

Describe *why* you are doing cell-based ministry.

What can you do to help more leaders grasp the why of small group ministry.

Define *empowerment* in your own words.

What steps can you take to empower your leaders more effectively.

Suggested Reading

Books

- Chapter 2-3 of *Leadership Explosion: Multiplying Cell Group Leaders for the Harvest* (2022 version)
- Chapter 5 of *How to be a Great Cell Group Coach* (2022 version)

Internet articles

Train Everyone to Make Disciples
Long-term Discipleship
The Coaching Tool box

Download this PowerPoint

Joel Comiskey's PowerPoint on this lesson:

https://tinyurl.com/585ta97j

CHAPTER 7

Pre-Transition: Preparing Your Church for the Transition to Cell Church

WATCH THIS VIDEO ▶

https://youtu.be/XPYFW9mKzY0

Introduction

- I coached a Baptist pastor a while ago who was the 30th pastor in a 66-year-old church. Before he got there, the average tenure of a pastor was 1.5 years. The church was very traditional.

- When Bill started his transition, he talked about the values of small group ministry, like love and relational evangelism. He made sure he didn't talk about models. He didn't throw around foreign names like Yoido Full Gospel Church, Ralph Neighbour, or other small group gurus.
- He realized that change takes a long time so he lovingly guided the church to make key changes.

Three stages

- When we talk about making a transition to small group ministry, we are referring to three stages: Pre-transition, transition, and post-transition.
- Pre-transition involves preparing the ground and winning the hearts of people to successfully start the process.

Pre-Transition

- During the pre-transition process, I teach key principles that will help guide the transition.
- The principles I'm going to share don't need to happen in a particular order, like a 1,2,3

process. They are simply truths that will help make the transition successful.

Lead pastor and team leading the vision

The lead pastor and leadership team must be clear on where they are going. Hopefully, they are convinced that cell church is biblical and the best way to make disciples who make disciples.

It's not enough for the lead pastor to have the vision; the vision must have him. He needs to be ready to get involved, rather than delegating the vision to someone else.

If the pastor doesn't plan on staying in the church, it might not be the right time to make a cell church transition.

Win those with influence in your church

Every church has movers and shakers. They have paid the price and believe in the church's mission. These people want to offer their input and the pastor needs to win them before starting the transition.

The pastor needs to graciously and patiently explain the *why* behind cell church ministry and why he wants the church to go in this direction. Explaining the biblical base and the key values or principles of cell church ministry will help a lot. Taking these key leaders to a cell-based church would also be helpful.

Finding the Needs in Your Own Church

Knowing the needs in your church will help you to zero in on how cell church ministry can meet those needs. For example, if the church lacks community, cell groups will strengthen the love and relational ties between the members.

If the church is lacking in evangelism, relational evangelism through cell groups will help the church move forward. Applying God's Word is another strong factor in favor of cell group ministry.

Learn from other cell churches

Visiting one or more cell-based churches will help the pastor and key leaders to grasp the possibilities. To know that other churches have successfully transition will give confidence and hope for the future.

Envision what you want to become

In the pre-transition stage, the pastor and team dreams of what the church could become. The danger is clinging to unrealistic expectations, but it's great to dream about what God might do through cell church ministry.

Understanding Key discoveries of change

Everett Rogers has written an important book, *Diffusion of Innovation,* on how change takes place in an organization. Roger's book is a textbook on change. He lists key aspects of change.

Compatibility

In the pre-transition stage, the pastor needs to talk about how the cell church will mesh with the church's previous values and traditions. Was the church a mission-driven church? Talk about how cell groups will more fully integrate with the mission vision. Is the church an evangelistic church? Talk about how cell groups reach out and meet needs in the neighborhood and city. Community? Cell groups will help the church practice the one-anothers of Scripture.

Don't talk about techniques or models from other churches. Don't talk about paradigm shifts or other scary concepts.

Advantage

The lead pastor and team must talk about the advantages of cell church. No pun intended but "sell" them on "cell church." Talk about how cell ministry will help the church become all God intended them to be.

Observability

Observability means that people want to see and experience cell church before they buy in completely. That's why starting with a pilot group is essential. When the people see the value changes and can experience the values, they are more likely to embrace the changes.

I tell churches to start with a pilot group so the key leaders can understand in a very practical way where they are going and what the next step holds.

Change takes time

Get ready for the long haul. Some experts say that a normal transition takes between 3-5 years—especially if the church has been around for a long time. If the pastor is the founding pastor, he is at a great advantage and the transition will take less time.

Church plants can start right away as a cell church because they have not collected years of tradition.

Many churches, however, need to count the cost of long-term change. Bobby Clinton, my professor of a change dynamic course at Fuller Theological Seminary, said something like, "Change takes longer than you think even when you are prepared for it to take a long time."

Social relationships

Everett Rogers brings out the importance of social relationships in change. People are not influenced by experts as much as friends. Be a friend. Take long walks or chats over coffee. Carefully explain the process of becoming a cell church.

Reinvention

Every church is unique and will make adaptations. Without adjustments, cell church ministry will rarely become a core part of the church culture. Expect adjustments and be willing to allow the church to make cell church ministry their own.

Conclusion

The role of leadership is to encourage throughout the change process. Sometimes things get worse before they get better. Often the church cannot see the overall progress. It's like flying a plane through the fog. The pilot depends 100% on the control panel. We have God's Word as our guide and confidence that the Holy Spirit will illuminate the process and help us to successfully make the transition.

Reflection Questions

What did you learn from this lesson?

What are the three transition stages that Comiskey talks about in this chapter? What stage is your church in right now?

Of all the change principles that Roger's has identified, which one does your church need to practice the most? Why?

Suggested Reading

Books

- Chapter 14 of Reap the Harvest: How a Small Group System Can Grow Your Church
- Chapter 11 of Myths and Truths of the Cell Church: Key Principles that Make or Break Cell Ministry

Internet articles

Planning for the Transition
Don't Start the Transition Immediately
Understand the Why Before Transitioning
How Change Works
Transition Takes Time

Download this PowerPoint

Joel Comiskey's PowerPoint on this lesson:

https://tinyurl.com/2swks76w

CHAPTER 8

Transition and Post-transition: Starting and Finishing Well

WATCH THIS VIDEO ▶

https://youtu.be/sBCXlwKF3l4

T ransitioning to the cell church vision is not an easy task.

Three stages of a successful transition

Successful cell church transitions go through three phases:

- Pre-transition
- Post-transition
- Transition

During the pre-transition, the pastor and key leaders prepare the people through preaching, personal communication, and teaching key cell church principles—especially focusing on the biblical base for cell group ministry.

Go-for-it Approach

I've noticed two ways to transition in my research of worldwide cell churches. The first I called the *go-for-it approach*. In this approach, the lead pastor starts a number of small groups at the same time.

For example, Sergio Solorzano, founding pastor of the Elim Church in San Salvador, returned from Yoido Full Gospel Church in South Korea in 1986 and asked all the pastors of small churches throughout San Salvador to close down and become one large city cell church. Pastor Solorzano had the authority to start many cells at once since he was the founding pastor of the Elim Church.

We already had twenty-one healthy cell groups when we started our transition in Quito, Ecuador, so our transition consisted in encouraging all the pastors to personally lead a cell and to oversee the twenty-one existing cells.

If you are planting a cell church, you can start immediately with cell groups because you will plant the first cell.

Model Cell Approach

I recommend the model cell or pilot group for most churches.

Let me give you an up-to-date example.

When we started helping Moses and Ingrid Valentin at New Beginnings Church in Los Angeles, California in 2019, Moses talked about starting six groups simultaneously. He had been preparing key leaders for several years. I suggested, however, that we begin with a single pilot group.

Moses wisely gathered the future teams together at his house to ensure they agreed to work together. We tried to fit future cell team leaders into units compatible with personality and giftings, but it didn't always work out the way we wanted.

In March 2019, we gathered these key leaders at Moses and Ingrid's home. We modeled a normal cell group from 7 p.m. to 8:30 p.m. The order:

- Icebreaker: fun and dynamic as opposed to a Bible exam

- Worship (normally youTube with sprinkled praise and prayer)
- Cell lesson based on the Sunday sermon. We followed three questions:
  - What does this passage say? (read the passage and have a time of silence before answering the question)
  - What is God saying to me through this passage? (read the passage and have a time of silence before answering the question)
  - How can I apply this passage during the next week? (read the passage and have a time of silence before answering the question)
- Prayer in smaller groups or one large group

At the end of each pilot group session, we had a debriefing time, where we shared mainly positive aspects of the meeting but also offered suggestions.

Moses and Ingrid led in their home for two months, and then we rotated among the various team leader's homes. The team leaders led the icebreaker, worship, lesson, and prayer. Everyone participated in the debriefing afterward.

Rotating in different homes was very important to see how the teams hosted the cell group, arranged the chairs, dealt with children, managed the refreshment time, and so forth.

After nine months, we were ready to multiply. We announced the five groups in January 2020 in front of the church, and they started their face-to-face groups. Then Covid-19 hit one month later! But they were ready, and we immediately broke up into Zoom cells and didn't miss a beat.

In one year, we multiplied to ten groups and then fourteen. We are now completely back to face-to-face groups.

Key Pilot Group Principles

- The only ones invited to the pilot group are those willing to lead their groups after the pilot group is over (in leadership teams).
- Pilot group members should be evangelizing but bringing the fruit of their evangelism to their new cells with them when they multiply. In the meantime, they can be personally following up on those who receive Jesus but not invite them back to the pilot group.
- Those leading the pilot group are facilitators, not Bible teachers. Cell leaders should talk 30% of the time and allow others to talk 70% of the time.

Post-transition

After the model cell multiplies, the church is encouraged to join one of the new cells.

The lead pastor and wife should lead an open cell after the transition. Staying in the battle and experiencing what the rest of the church experiences is essential.

Moses and Ingrid Valentin continue to lead an open-cell group to this day. My wife and I lead an open cell.

The lead pastor and wife coach those leading cells until supervisors are formed. I think a ratio of one supervisor to three cells is the best ratio—while the supervisor continues to lead an open cell.

During the post-transition, the church perfects the equipping track, which the entire church should take. The equipping path does not take place during the cell. Remember, the cell lesson is based on the pastor's sermon, and I recommend following three simple questions that I mentioned earlier in this lesson.

The equipping track lasts from four months to one year and covers basic doctrines, freedom in Jesus, how to have daily devotions, evangelism, and leading a cell group. Some churches run their equipping track before or after the worship service or via Zoom.

I encourage churches to place a cell map in the church so that people can see where the cell groups are meeting. Many cell churches arrange their offices to better care for the cell groups. I encourage churches to allow people to see inward-cell values outwardly (maps, banners, offices, etc.).

Some experts say transitioning from an established church to a cell-based church takes about five years.

Get ready for the long haul. But if you start well, you'll continue to grow and develop. God will help you to make disciples who make disciples for his glory.

Reflection Questions

What did you learn from this lesson?

Why is it important to start with a pilot group when making the transition?

What post-transition action is the most important for your church right now?

Where are you in the transition process and what area needs the most attention?

Suggested Reading

Books

- *Chapter 15 of Reap the Harvest: How a Small Group System Can Grow Your Church*

Internet articles

Starting with a Pilot Group
Modeling Cell Ministry through a Pilot Group
Post-transition: Building the Components

Download this PowerPoint

Joel Comiskey's PowerPoint on this lesson:

https://tinyurl.com/2d66hp38

CHAPTER 9

Discipleship Equipping: Making Disciples through Specific Training

WATCH THIS VIDEO ▶

https://youtu.be/qqtVKqbIfcw

I n the book of Mark, we see that Jesus spent 49% of his time with his disciples and 51% with the multitude.

Jesus knew that the disciples would continue his ministry and change the world. Therefore, he spent quality time with them.

Cell church ministry is all about making disciples who make disciples. The goal is to prepare harvest workers who will do the work of the ministry. The cell church strategy does this by asking each member to participate in a cell and practice the one another's of the Bible. Each member also attends the Sunday celebration service to hear the Word of God, worship, and fellowship with all the cell members. Those leading cell groups receive close supervision, which helps in the discipleship process.

But there's more. Cell churches also have equipping tracks to train each member and take them to the next level. The preaching of the Word is essential in the discipleship process, but gaps remain. For example, members need to learn how to evangelize, have their devotional time, receive freedom from addictions and other bondages, and facilitate a small group.

Duration of the Basic Equipping

In my investigation of equipping tracks worldwide, I noticed that the church-wide equipping lasted four months to one year. Everyone in the church was encouraged to take the equipping. These churches had only one equipping track but featured many methods to complete the equipping (e.g., one-on-one, one-on-two, classrooms, retreats, etc.).

Equipping names

Churches use different names to describe their equipping, such as the school of leaders, Bible Academy, training track, or route. I often use *discipleship equipping* to remember the reason for the equipping: make disciples. Jesus gave his church the great commission in Matthew 28:18-20 and teaching them to observe everything was part of that commission.

Great Equipping Tracks

I consider Ralph Neighbour, the guru of cell ministry. He's over 90 years old and continues to minister and counsel cell churches. He has written best-selling books on the cell church movement and an excellent equipping track lasting one year. In Neighbour's equipping, a person starts in the cell group and is assigned a mentor who takes them through the *Arrival Kit*. The unique part of Neighbour's training is connecting the teaching with cell life. Neighbour combines weekend retreats with personal study.

Little Falls Christian Center asked Neighbour for permission to reduce the training to four months.

The new believer starts the process with the *Welcome to Your Changed Life* booklet. Three more manuals follow until the person leads a cell group or is part of a cell team. The church offers an upper -level training for those who are leading a cell group or part of a leadership team.

Bethany World Prayer Center has adjusted its training many times over the years. They originally designed their discipleship equipping in the form of a baseball diamond. A person started in a cell as they headed toward first base. Along the way, they were baptized in water. Discipleship 101 discussed the basics of the faith and Discipleship 201 (2nd base) and 301 (3rd base) delved deeper into doctrine and spiritual disciplines. A homerun was participating in cell leadership. Bethany had additional training for those leading cell groups.

I tell pastors and leaders to start with someone else's equipping with the goal of developing their discipleship equipping. A church should include its vision, doctrine, and unique identity.

Steal the Best with Pride

I've fulfilled my counsel in my equipping track. Previously, I would recommend one book from Neighbour and another from someone else. Eventually, I created my own discipleship equipping, which lasts for nine months.

- The first book is Live (8 weeks). The purpose is to teach the basics of the Christian faith and help the person understand the plan of salvation. Live talks about prayer, reading the Word, and other Christian disciplines.
- Encounter (8 weeks) helps a new believer receive freedom from addictions and bondages.
- Grow (8 weeks) guides the Christian to have a daily quiet time.
- Share (8 weeks) instructs the believer on how to share Jesus with others.
- Facilitate (8 weeks) prepares the believers to facilitate a cell group or be part of a cell team.

Clarity and Specificity

All of the discipleship training was clear and specific. People knew how to start and when to finish.

On the other hand, education in many churches has no starting point or end. Class after class is added to the mix. I heard of a Texas church asking members to take 435 hours of classroom discussion. As a result of the education, people can become parking lot attendants or part of the yearly pageant. In other words, this church featured lots of education but little application.

Cell churches, on the other hand, equip God's people to minister in a cell group and pastor the members.

Remember that education lasts a lifetime, but equipping is for a specific task. Neil McBride distinguishes the two:

> Education is an expanding activity; starting with where a person is at, it provides concepts and information for developing broader perspectives and the foundations for making future analysis and decisions. On the other hand, training is a narrowing activity; given whatever a person's present abilities are, it attempts to provide specific skills and the necessary understanding to apply those skills. The focus is on accomplishing a specific task or job (*How to Build a Small Groups Ministry*, p. 128).

The discipleship equipping in cell churches is specific and concrete. It prepares believers for service.

I pray that you will have a new vision to prepare the laypeople to do the work of the ministry. I've updated my book *Leadership Explosion* in 2022. In this

book, I talk about the principles behind discipleship
equipping and give examples of effective discipleship equipping.

Reflection Questions

What did you learn from this lesson?

In your own words, what is the difference between
education and equipping?

What can you do to improve your equipping track?

Suggested Reading

Books

- Chapters 9-10 of *Leadership Explosion:
  Multiplying Cell Group Leaders to Reap the
  Harvest*

Internet articles

Train Everyone to Make Disciples
Discipleship Equipping
Differences between Education and Equipping
Joel Comiskey's Equipping Track

Download this PowerPoint

Joel Comiskey's PowerPoint on this lesson:

https://tinyurl.com/yf2cwktx

CHAPTER 10

The Principles Behind the Best Equipping Tracks

WATCH THIS VIDEO ▶

https://youtu.be/B6oIR93oE-o

F ollow principles, not models. Following principles not only apply to the general cell structure but also to the equipping track.

I've noticed at least seven principles behind the best equipping tracks. I highlight these principles in my book *Leadership Explosion* (2022 edition).

Principle #1: Keep the Training Track Simple

Many pastors and leaders make their equipping too complicated. They try to add too much training in the basic training, and the equipping takes years to complete. I encourage leaders to have a basic level for those preparing to become disciple-makers (part of a cell leadership team or the point person on the leadership team) and an advanced level for those in the battle.

A typical equipping track takes about six months and no more than one year. Nine months works well.

The first manual should cover fundamental doctrine and spiritual disciplines: salvation by grace (and steps for a person to receive Jesus), how to read the Bible, how to pray, baptism, Jesus as Lord, the Lord's supper, and the importance of giving (tithing/offering).

The second manual covers how to be free from sins like unforgiveness, rejection, and other addictions.

The third manual is how to have a daily quiet time. It's not enough to feed the person. We must teach them how to feed themselves; I believe that daily quiet time is the most important discipline in the Christian life.

The fourth manual should cover how to evangelize. Many believers know how to share their testimonies, but the manual on evangelism gives the person a step-by-step guide on how to share the gospel.

The fifth manual teaches how to facilitate a small group. Everyone should be prepared to be a disciple-maker and be ready to be part of a leadership team, if not the point person in the small group.

Principle #2: Provide Action Steps with the Training

The equipping must go beyond learning and involve action. For example, the person should be baptized after graduating from the first book about Christianity 101.

In the second manual about spiritual freedom, the person needs to confess and renounce sins and receive the Spirit's filling.

The third manual covers personal daily devotions, and the person needs to start practicing daily devotions.

The fourth manual is about evangelism, and the person needs to practice sharing the gospel.

The fifth manual covers facilitating a cell group, and the person should practice leading each part of the cell with the hope of being part of a cell leadership team.

Principle #3: Prepare the Second Level of Training for Cell Leaders

The best cell churches continually prepare those leading a cell group or part of a leadership team. I've known churches that had upper levels of leadership equipping that prepared the leaders to become church planters and pastors.

In my upper-level equipping, I have three books: *Lead, Coach,* and *Discover.* You can be creative in preparing your upper-level training and teach material like *spiritual warfare* or deeper-level doctrine.

Principle #4: Use Only One Equipping Track

Each church needs to decide what its church-wide equipping will be. Having one training track for the youth and another for the children's leaders is not wise. It's best to have only one church-wide equipping and then to make adjustments for different age groups without changing the core teachings.

Principle #5: There is No One Methodology for Implementing Your Training

I've been in churches that tried to tie the training methodology with the equipping track. In other words, they said everyone had to go through the equipping one-on-one, no questions asked. Yet, in my research, many churches used the classroom setting for equipping.

I counsel churches to offer various possibilities to equip the people. For example, churches might prepare their people during the "Sunday school" as the main way to train people. Yet, there's nothing wrong with using an entire Saturday to go through one manual. And if someone can't make it to either of these two options, maybe they can meet personally with someone from the cell before or after the cell meeting.

Principle #6: Train Everyone to Become a Disciple-Maker

The equipping is not just for cell leadership but for everyone. The goal is to make disciples of the entire church; thus, everyone must go through the equipping. Not everyone will be the main leader of a cell, but everyone should prepare to be part of a leadership team.

Principle #7: Continually Adjust and Improve the Training

Don't expect perfection immediately. You'll need to adjust and adapt. You might find the need to change the material or add additional training. You'll need to look for the best times to implement the training. In other words, don't expect overnight success. But don't wait.

God wants to make disciples of all nations. He wants to use you and your church to prepare disciples who make disciples. The equipping track is part of the discipleship process, and as you equip your entire church, you'll discover new leadership possibilities.

Reflection Questions

What did you learn from this lesson?
What principle is your church doing the best at?
What principle does your church need to implement?

Suggested Reading

Books

- Chapter 11 of *Leadership Explosion: Multiplying Cell Group Leaders to Reap the Harvest*

Internet articles

Principles of the Best Equipping Tracks
Different Ways to Teach the Discipleship Equipping
The Place of Encounter Retreats in the Equipping

Download this PowerPoint

Joel Comiskey's PowerPoint on this lesson:

https://tinyurl.com/w2xrtspe

CHAPTER 11

Why Supervision (coaching) is so Important in Cell Church Ministry

WATCH THIS VIDEO ▶

https://youtu.be/ezflRrFNMYw

One pastor recently shared his love for the cell church structure and its effectiveness. He said that early in his ministry, he started many small groups that caused division in his church. So why was he so excited now? One key reason was the coaching structure. Now, the church had a system of supervisors to care for the small groups.

A good friend, Jim Egli, surveyed 3000 cell group leaders and discovered coaching was the number one factor behind successful small group-based churches.

David Cho, the founder of the largest church in the world, once said that supervisors held the most crucial role in his church. But why is this?

Reasons for Coaching

What do coaches do that makes them so valuable in the cell church system?

Coaches pray for the leaders.

Coaches pray for the leaders and create a prayer shield around the leader. They enter the spiritual battle on the leader's behalf, making a huge difference.

Coaches Help Prevent Problems

They get to know the leaders and can catch problems before they become a major crisis. I'm referring to sin problems and rebellion. But the coach also encourages the leader and constantly looks for ways to pinpoint positive traits.

Coaching allows less mature leaders to facilitate groups

I remember when I first started studying the Elim Church. They released leaders after a very short time of training. The reason they were so successful was because of their excellent system of coaching. The supervisors would review the lesson with the leaders and then visit the cell group to ensure quality.

Content of Coaching

More than structure is the content of coaching. I have several books on this issue that will help you further. My book *How to Be a Great Cell Group Coach* gives insights into coaching leaders more effectively. *Coach* is a teaching manual on how to coach leaders. My book, *You Can Coach,* also talks about the content of coaching.

Principles of Coaching

I recommend key **fundamental principles** for coaching leaders:

Receive

Effective coaches first receive from Jesus. They are filled with the Spirit and spend time with Jesus before trying to coach the leader. They also make sure they have their day off and are first focusing on their inner circle (spouse, family, close friends). They can then minister more effectively to those they are coaching.

Listen

Fruitful coaching is more about listening than talking. Leaders have to deal with many issues and need someone to be there. When I first started coaching, I thought my role was to give counsel, but I soon found out that leaders were more interested in a listening ear. They wanted to talk. Wise supervisors prepare powerful questions and then listen intently to the leaders. They allow the leaders to share their stories instead of discussing their own.

Encourage

It's not easy to lead a cell group. Leaders often become discouraged when they expect more people to attend the small group and far fewer people arrive. Encouragement helps the leader to press ahead. Supervisors can remind the leaders about their eternal rewards to continue making disciples for God's glory.

Care

Supervisors serve the leaders rather than control them. They meet their needs, knowing that the leaders care for the flock. Remember that Jesus washed the feet of the disciples. He cared for them. He even called them friends. In John 15:15, Jesus said, "I no longer call you servants but friends." The best coaches become friends with the cell leader, breaking down walls through a loving, caring atmosphere.

Develop

Development is different than training. Everyone in the church undergoes the training and receives the same information. Development, however, focuses on the needs of the particular leader. It pinpoints what the leader needs. For example, perhaps the supervisor notices the leader needs more help listening, asking questions, or developing new leaders. The coach can help the leader in that particular area by recommending a video, article, book, or seminar.

Strategize

Coaches help the leaders reach out, identify new leaders, and prepare for multiplication. Often, the coach will help the leader remember overlooked members or ask the leader why a particular cell member has not started the equipping. Another strategy issue is ensuring the leader hands in the cell report which helps everyone in the church strategize more effectively to make disciples who make quality disciples.

Challenge

Coaches encourages leaders to fulfill God's vision for the cell. The coach challenges the leaders to fulfill the great commission, making disciples who make disciples.

Another aspect of challenging is to speak the hard truth at times. Perhaps the supervisor notices a dullness in the leader, so she says, "Can I share something with you?" The leader will reply yes. "How is your quiet time?" "Are you spending regular time with Jesus?" Or "How is your marriage doing?" "How can I help?"

Conclusion

Coaching is the glue of cell church ministry. Effective coaching helps leaders more effectively make disciples who make disciples. Cell churches with effective coaching avoid the dangers and pitfalls of division. God wants your church to have a solid coaching structure.

Reflection Questions

What did you learn from this lesson?

Comiskey talks about various reasons for coaching. What reason stood out to you the most?

Why does Comiskey say that the content of the coaching is more important than the structure?

What is the coaching principle that you need to work on the most?

Suggested Reading

Books

- Chapters 1-7 of *How to Be a Great Cell Group Coach: Practical Insight for Supporting and Mentoring Cell Group*
- Chapter 1-9 of *Coach: Empower Others to Effectively Lead a Small Group*
- Chapter 10 of *Myths and Truths of the Cell Church: Key Principles that Make or Break Cell Ministry*

Internet articles

Key Coaching Principles
Use Everything in the Toolbox
How to Encourage Your Leaders
What the Best Coaches Do

Download this PowerPoint

Joel Comiskey's PowerPoint on this lesson:

https://tinyurl.com/5n7c9was

CHAPTER 12

Coaching Visitation, Frequency, and Models

WATCH THIS VIDEO ▶

https://youtu.be/aQ50GHSyH2Q

S omeone has said you must fail at least three times in cell ministry to get it right. I agree.

One of those failures occurred when I was part of a pastoral team. We decided we needed to do small groups. "Wasn't everyone doing them?" We identified some mature leaders and sent them out to lead small groups. We offered practically zero oversight and would occasionally hear a report about how they were doing. All of them failed.

I learned from that failure that coaching is essential to maintain small group momentum.

Visiting Cell Groups

One tried and true method of coaching is cell visitation. Supervisors visit the cell groups as members. Since the 1960s, when David Cho started his cell church structure in South Korea, small group visitation has played an important role. Before visiting, I encourage supervisors to:

- Let the leader know you'll be visiting beforehand. Some surprises are lovely but not the surprise of a supervisor showing up without proper notice.
- The supervisor in the group should act like an ordinary member, sharing transparently and not acting like someone critiquing the group.
- Compliment the small group leader afterward. Offer far more encouragements than critiques.
- If the supervisor needs to share a suggestion with the leader, it's best to begin with

the phrase, "Can I share something with you I noticed?" In other words, ask for permission.

While visiting is a great way to know what's going on in the groups, I believe that the supervisor's participation in a small group is even more critical. A supervisor at least needs to be in one small group as a member. I think it's even better if the supervisor leads a small group or is part of a small group team. And this is more and more common in cell churches worldwide.

Frequency of leadership meetings

How often should the supervisor meet with the leader? My observation is that a supervisor should meet with those leaders under their care one time per month as a group and then one time individually. The personal meeting might be a phone call, zoom meeting, meeting after church, or another type of contact. The group meeting might also be a Zoom meeting to share victories, needs, the health of the groups, and vision casting.

Let's say a pastor decides to start small groups with a pilot group. The pastor leads the pilot group for six months to a year. Let's say that four groups multiply from the pilot group. The pastor would coach those four leaders (or leadership teams), asking them to meet once monthly as a group of leaders. Those meetings might take place on Zoom (or another App) or face-to-face.

The pastor would also individually contact those leaders to serve and care for them during the month.

When the number of cells reache seven to ten, the pastor would need to develop two supervisors, each taking four to five groups (I believe a ratio of 1 to 3 is ideal). The pastor would then concentrate on those supervisors who would care for the cell leaders.

Different models of coaching

Jethro Model

A common type of cell coaching is called the 5x5 or Jethro Model. A supervisor takes care of five cell leaders. A zone pastor takes care of five supervisors, and a district pastor oversees the approximately five zone pastors. These numbers are not exact, but they generally follow the advice that Jethro gave to Moses, "Moses listened to his father-in-law and did everything he said. He chose capable men from all Israel and made them leaders of the people, officials over thousands, hundreds, fifties and tens" (Exodus 18:24–25).

I wrote a book called *Passion and Persistence,* in which I analyzed the Elim Church in El Salvador, who follow the 5X5 precisely. They organize their cell structure geographically, so it's straightforward to follow. They have section leaders (supervisors over five groups), zone pastors (those pastors over supervisors), and district pastors (those caring for the zone pastors). These supervisors have come through the system and are raised up based on their character and fruit.

G-12 Model

The G12 Model came out of Bogota, Colombia. It's an adaptation of the 5X5 model. G12 isn't organized geographically but in homogenous networks. They follow two fundamental principles:

- Every person is a potential leader
- Every leader is a potential supervisor

In the G12 model, the goal of each leader is to multiply their cell twelve times while continuing to lead their cell group.

I don't recommend G12 for two reasons:

1. For laypeople to lead a cell while caring for twelve leaders is way too much and promotes burnout
2. The G12 model that came out of Bogota asked all churches to follow their model exactly—to adopt rather than adapt. By trying to control churches, many divisions occurred worldwide.

G12.3

I promote following principles rather than models. My adaptation is the G12.3 model. In this model, a full-time pastor might coach up to 12 leaders, but a layperson should have the goal of coaching a maximum of three leaders while continuing to lead their cell group.

I believe this is far more manageable, doable, and works in practice.

If the leader cannot coach while leading a cell for lack of time, the pastor appoints a supervisor to coach that new leader. The reality is this: there is no perfect model, including G12.3.

Keep the focus on making disciples

Pastor, Jesus wants to use you and your church to make disciples who make disciples. Just remember that establishing a solid coaching structure is essential and helps fulfill the great commission.

Reflection Questions

What did you learn from this lesson?

What did you learn from this lesson about visiting cell groups? How will you change from what you learned?

How often do you coach your leaders? What do you need to do differently?

What coaching model most resembles what you are doing in your church? What do you need to change?

Suggested Reading

Books

- *Chapter 10 of Reap the Harvest: Making Disciples through Holistic Small Group Ministry*
- *Chapter 11-12 of How to Be a Great Cell Group Coach: Practical Insight for Supporting and Mentoring Cell Group*
- *Chapters 3,9 of You Can Coach: How to Help Leaders Build Healthy Churches Through Coaching*

Internet articles

Common Coaching Structures
Strengths and Weaknesses of Coaching Structures
G 12.3 Coaching Structure
How to Structure Coaching, part 1
How to Structure Coaching, part 2

Download this PowerPoint

Joel Comiskey's PowerPoint on this lesson:

https://tinyurl.com/bdcmamt4

CHAPTER 13

Key Principles of Simple Cell Church Planting

WATCH THIS VIDEO ▶

https://youtu.be/7duNAt0Cyso

I remember ministering in a church in Florida a few years ago. The pastors on the team asked me questions about their cell group networks. They wanted to know who would coach the new leaders after they multiplied to the third and fourth generations. I tried to answer their questions, thinking I had studied mega-cell churches and should know the answers. But I finally blurted out, "You need to plant new churches." In other words, I felt their situations had become complicated as they grew. Church planting brings the church back to a simpler, more reproducible state.

New Testament church planting was simple and reproducible. Paul and others planted small reproducible house-based churches throughout the then-known world. The Roman authorities couldn't snuff them out.

I do believe that some cell churches will grow to mega-church status, but the vast majority will be much smaller. Jesus desires to multiply laborers at all levels: cell, supervisor, and pastoral. We need also to release church planters and missionaries. Sadly, some large cell churches want to keep pastors and leaders in their large mega-church structure rather than releasing them to plant new churches.

But what is a New Testament church? Before talking about planting New Testament churches, we need to ask the question about what they are. The New Testament contains some basic features of simple, reproducible cell churches.

What is the Local Church?
Under the Lordship of Jesus

The New Testament *ecclesia* gathered under the direction of Jesus Christ. Many verses in the New Testament talk about Jesus as the head of the church. Romans 14 and Philippians 2 tell us that every knee will bow and proclaim that Jesus is Lord. The gathered church is not a club. Instead, it's a gathered assembly under the Lordship of Jesus.

Directed by God-ordained Leadership

Hebrews 13:17 tells us that we must submit to those God has placed over us. Jesus, the head of the church, develops godly leaders to guide his church. We read the same thing in Ephesians 4. He gives gifted men and women to bless and guide his church.

A Particular Location

Scripture talks about the church at Corinth or Rome. It also talks about the church in the house of Maria or Priscilla and Aquilla. In other words, we regularly read about the church meeting at a particular place and time. Yes, it's true that whenever two or three are gathered in Christ's name, he is in the midst of them. However, the local church is different. We see a permanency and consistency of God's people meeting together.

Partaking in the Sacraments

The Bible speaks of two sacraments—Baptism and the Lord's Supper. The local church regularly guides and participates in these two sacraments.

What does it take to plant a New Testament Church?

I've noticed some necessary characteristics for fruitful church planters.

Godly character

Scripture talks about leadership characteristics in 1 Timothy 3 and Titus 1. I like how D.L. Moody once described godly leadership. He said godly leadership is what you do in the dark when no one else is looking. God sees.

A great relationship with the spouse

The great apostle Paul was never married, and planting a church as a single person is undoubtedly an option. But if the church planter is married, both husband and wife must agree about planting the church. I've seen church plants fail when only one spouse feels a calling to plant the church.

Calling

I believe anyone can facilitate a small group or be part of a leadership team. However, pastoring a New Testament church plant requires a particular calling. The church planting pastor is responsible under God for those in the church. The buck stops with the church planter.

Fruitfulness

Those who plant successful cell churches have led and multiplied cell groups before becoming church planters. The process is straightforward and concise: lead a cell, multiply the cell, supervise the fruit of multiplication, get more training, and then plant a cell church.

Future church planters gather vital experience from leading and multiplying cell groups. I talked to one church planter who was planting a church in Bangladesh. He was showing me his plans to start a celebration service because he already had several cell groups functioning. What was interesting to me was that this church planter was first a fruitful cell leader and supervisor in Hong Kong. The Hong Kong church had seen his fruit and character and then sent him to plant a cell church in Bangladesh.

Jesus desires to develop workers for his harvest. Cell church planting is at the heart of what Jesus is doing worldwide.

Reflection Questions

What did you learn from this lesson?

What did you learn about the nature of the local church from this lesson?

Comiskey talks about important characteristics for those who would plant a simple NT church. What stands out to you as the most?

How is God calling you to participate in church planting?

Suggested Reading

Books

- Chapters 2-7 of *Planting Churches that Reproduce: Starting a Network of Simple Churches*
- Chapter 12 of *Myths and Truths of the Cell Church: Key Principles that Make or Break Cell Ministry*

Internet articles

What is a Simple Cell Church?
How Cell Multiplication Prepares Church Planters
Important Qualities of Church Planters
Paul's Method of Church Planting
Planting New Testament Cell Churches
Mega Church Myths

Download this PowerPoint

Joel Comiskey's PowerPoint on this lesson:

https://tinyurl.com/2p9mf8ve

CHAPTER 14

Steps to Simple Cell Church Planting

WATCH THIS VIDEO ▶

https://youtu.be/WnmSsqN-Cic

W hat does it take to plant a simple, reproducible cell church? Here are essential principles.

Recruit Prayer Partners

Church planters enter enemy territory and can expect resistance. Satan hates those who win souls to Jesus and develop new leaders. Thus, before starting the church planting process, its essential to gather a team of prayer warriors who will act as a prayer shield.

Paul the apostle is our example here. He was constantly asking others to pray for him. Notice what he said:

- "Brothers, pray for us" (1 Thessalonians 5:25)
- "Now I be you, brothers, through the Lord Jesus Christ, and through the love of the Spirit, that you strive with me in your prayers to God for me" (Romans 15:30).
- "I trust that through your prayers I shall be granted to you" (Philemon 22)

I always recommend C. Peter Wagner's book *Prayer Shield*, which talks about gathering and sustaining prayer partners.

Learn the Culture

Church planters should do everything possible to understand the people and culture where they will plant the church. I recommend doing a lot of prayer walking and talking to the people. Church planters can also gather loads of information from the Internet about every aspect of the culture where they will plant the church. Jesus is our example. He became God incarnate and walked among a particular culture. We must also be Christ's hands and feet to those God has called us to serve.

Develop a team

I do not believe in lone-ranger church planters. Paul had a team, as did Jesus. Leadership in the New Testament is always plural. Church planters need to have like-minded fellow workers with whom they can minister.

Of course, it'd be wonderful if the mother church could provide people and a team for the church plant. I was involved in one church plant where the mother church gave 150 people and ten cell groups to plant a daughter church plant. We were running from the very beginning.

Yet, many church planters will start with a team and plant the first cell.

The first cell group is the church.

The Bible identifies many house churches. We read about the church in the house of Mary or the house of Pricilla and Aquila. In other words, the cell is the church.

Many who write about church planting talk about the big launch as *starting the church*. Cell church planting is different. The first cell is the church.

Multiply the first cell.

The goal of the church planter is to multiply the first cell and continue the multiplication process. The church planter becomes the coach of the new cells and new cell leaders.

Start the first celebration service.

I caution church planters not to start the first service immediately. Wait until there are enough cells and momentum.

I recommend waiting until there are two or three active cell groups and then gathering those cells into a once-per-month celebration service—preaching, worship, and so forth.

Then, when there are four to five cell groups, gather them together twice monthly. When there are about eight cells and 70+ people to have weekly Sunday celebration gatherings.

Unlike traditional church planting, cell church planting focuses on the organic house-to-house ministry. I call it the cell-driven strategy. In the meantime, all the people can gather for prayer, training, and social gatherings.

I've talked to many church planters who lament that they started their Sunday celebration gathering too early. They could never get beyond the small celebration gathering, and they put all their focus and energy into getting the celebration service off the ground. They neglected the cells and stagnated.

Multiply Churches

Jesus told us to make disciples of all nations (Matthew 28:18-20). He desires to develop laborers who will reap the harvest. Church planting is at the forefront of making disciples and reaching a lost world for Jesus.

Reflection Questions

What did you learn from this lesson?

What step stood out to you as the most important?

How can you be involved in church planting?

Suggested Reading

Books

- *Chapters 8-10 of Planting Churches that Reproduce: Starting a Network of Simple Churches*

Internet articles

How to Plant a Cell Church?
How to Plant a House Church?
Snapshot of Church Planting
Church Planting: the Heart of the Great Commission

Download this PowerPoint

Joel Comiskey's PowerPoint on this lesson:

https://tinyurl.com/4pfpywhe

CHAPTER 15

Myths and Truths: Vision and Models

WATCH THIS VIDEO ▶

https://youtu.be/emwJmGiX3c0

C ell church is a biblically based strategy to make disciples who make disciples. I believe it's the best strategy to fulfill the great commission. Those taking the plunge into cell church ministry must also know the pitfalls and difficulties. My book *Myths and Truths of the Cell Church* identifies common myths and how to avoid them.

Vision Myths and Truths

Myth: The Cell church strategy is a mega-church strategy

The largest, most prominent churches in the world are cell churches. We rejoice in their size and worldwide impact. Should all churches desire mega-church status?

Truth: Few Cell churches reach mega-church status

A tiny percentage of cell churches will grow to become mega-churches, and they are the exceptions rather than the rule. The reality is that the majority of worldwide cell churches are small and agile. They decide to plant new churches rather than grow larger and larger.

One of the modern church growth miracles is China, where the church has grown and expanded under the radar of the communist government. How has the Chinese church done this? House-to-house ministry.

The reality is that few leaders have the gifts and talents to administrate huge cell churches. Most pastors will choose the simple, reproducible cell church structure.

Myth: The Cell Church Does Not Work

Most pastors want their churches to grow faster than they are. They might become a cell church hoping to see more church growth and become disappointed when the results aren't more positive. They then say that cell church does not work. What they are usually saying, however, is that it did not work as quickly as expected.

Truth: Cell Church Brings Health, Life, and Growth

The cell church strategy helps a church grow in quality, resulting in numerical growth. Cell ministry stirs members to live out the message during the week, be accountable to a smaller group of believers, and receive training to become disciple-makers.

Natural Church Development did a comparative study of cell churches versus non-cell churches and discovered that cell churches were healthier in all eight NCD principles. Cell churches also grew 2.5 times faster. This particular NCD study used twenty million pieces of data to compare the growth rates of cell churches with non-cell churches, so the findings are significant.

But maybe you are not experiencing rapid growth and are wondering why your church growth is so slow. I want to encourage you to hang in there. God will give you the growth in his time.

Myth: Cell Church is a Fad

Truth: The Cell Church Has Deep Roots

Cell church ministry has deep biblical roots, starting with Jethro's advice to Moses in the Old Testament (Exodus 18). And the New Testament was a house-to-house movement. We cannot properly understand the New Testament without grasping the house-to-house context. Jesus lived, traveled, and ministered from house to house, sending his disciples into the homes to minister. They followed his example after Pentecost, and the early church was born as a house-to-house movement.

Cell church also has a long history in the Christian church. The Waldenses, Lollards, Hussites, and Moravians met in cell groups. Philip Spener (1666 AD), the founder of Pietism, would take his sermon notes and prepare carefully designed questions for his small group leaders. John Wesley carried the cell church model to another level, requiring those attending the society meetings to show proof they regularly attended their cell meetings. David Cho based his cell group ministry on New Testament principles, and the church grew to become the largest church in the history of Christianity.

I browsed the pages of a book in my library called *Cells for Life* by Ron Trudinger. I felt like I was reading a book written in 2024, but then I discovered that Trudginger's ministry happened in the 60s, and he wrote the book in 1979. Cell church ministry has deep roots and is far more than a fad.

Model Myths and Truths

Myth: Following a Particular Model Will Bring Success

Truth: Apply Principles to Your Specific Situation

A few years ago, I consulted a couple of pastors who came to my home to learn about cell church. They said, "We followed Bethany World Prayer Center exactly, and it didn't work. Then we tried the Rick Warren *Purpose Driven Church* model, which didn't bring fruit. Now we're trying G12, and it's not giving us the desired results. What should we do?

I didn't say it at the time, but later realized they were infected by what I call *model sickness*. It's the hope that following someone else's model will bring success. We must apply the principles from worldwide cell churches and not follow one particular model. Why? Our traditions, contexts, and personalities are distinct; only principles can effectively adapt to our particular situation.

Myth: Once You Have a Model, Stick by It

Truth: Innovate and Change the Model as the Spirit Leads

Those who create models can change them whenever the Spirit of God nudges them. Those who come along afterward must try to discern what changes the founders have made or are making. They always ask questions about what the model's founder is doing instead of what the Spirit of God wants them to do.

Allow the Spirit of God to guide you according to Biblical principles and common worldwide cell church principles. Avoid following models. Ask the Spirit for the power of creativity.

Myth: Cell Church Focuses Exclusively on the Cell and Celebration

Truth: The Cell Church Focuses on Key Systems that Produce Life in the Cell and Celebration

Cell church ministry is simple: cell, celebration, coaching, and equipping. All four of these aspects move the church forward to make more and better Christ-like disciples. Christ's goal is to make us like him.

Equipping people through biblically-based training develops future leaders. However, those leaders must also receive care and encouragement. Coaching is essential for cells to stay on the cutting edge. The cell and celebration provide the atmosphere where disciples grow and develop.

I pray you will stay on the cutting edge by avoiding the myths and applying the truths.

Reflection Questions

What did you learn from this lesson?

What was the myth/truth in this lesson that stood out to you?

Which myth/truth is God showing you to apply in your church?

Suggested Reading

Books

- *Chapter 1-2 of Myths and Truths of the Cell Church: Key Principles that Make or Break Cell Ministry*

Internet articles

Myths and Truths: The Cell Church Doesn't Work

The Myth of Cell Church as a Mega-Church Strategy

Myth: Leading People into Cell Church Is Similar to Leading People into Other Church Programs

Model Sickness: Problems of Trying to Imitate the Model Cell Church

Download this PowerPoint

Joel Comiskey's PowerPoint on this lesson:

https://tinyurl.com/4dzsnnss

CHAPTER 16

Myths and Truths: Church Growth and Leadership

WATCH THIS VIDEO ▶

https://youtu.be/sLF3q4ggZ0o

I remember one church that was a shining example of cell church ministry. This church was balanced and generous and held regular cell church conferences. The pastor, however, became attracted to one particular Latin American model and submitted himself and the church to follow that model. I didn't know the lead pastor well enough to talk with him, nor was he looking for my counsel.

Yet, I knew he was taking his church down the wrong path. This once-balanced cell church slowly lost its vision, direction, and vibrancy.

Let's look at some church growth myths and truths.

Church Growth Myths and Truths

Myth: Church Growth is the Driving Motivation for Becoming a Cell Church

Pastors and churches often become excited about cell church ministry because of the possibilities of church growth. But what happens if they have unfulfilled expectations? Follow a better, more exciting model?

Truth: Theology is the True Foundation upon Which to Build a Cell Church

The correct motivation for cell church ministry is the biblical base. Theology breeds methodology. God will give growth in his timing, but when we know we're doing the right thing, we can keep pressing ahead despite obstacles and setbacks. Why? Because we know we are making disciples of Jesus Christ and following biblical principles.

Knowing that theology breeds methodology will help us be patient until Jesus bears the fruit in his time. We won't strive to perform an artificial church growth timeline, often producing weak, manufactured cell groups.

We should continually pray for abundant fruit and play an intricate role in producing it. Nevertheless, God must give the growth, and he will do so in his timing.

Myth: If I Choose to Become a Cell Church, My Church Will Grow

Cell church ministry is not a magical formula or a 1,2,3 technique, even though many view it as such.

Truth: Only Jesus Can Give True Organic Growth

The reality is that only Jesus Christ can produce true growth. After all, it's his church and not ours.

A few years ago, I was walking on the sands of Myrtle Beach, South Carolina. At the time, I was wrestling internally with cell church issues, and I envisioned the cell church like a giant kite stranded on the sand. As I mulled over the image of a colossal kite stranded on the sand, I thought, *Kites are supposed to fly freely in the air.* This kite, however, was stuck on the sand. Then, I pondered the reality that without a burst of wind, kites cannot fly.

Apart from the wind of the Spirit, a cell church is simply a structure stranded on the sand. It won't go anywhere, nor can it. Many books have expounded on the cell church structure, and yes, it's essential to have a structure to coach and train leaders effectively. But far more important is the wind of the Holy Spirit, who must breathe life into the cells and church.

I gave a seminar in New Jersey in a small, vibrant cell church that had plateaued. However, the pastor was discouraged because his church was not growing as envisioned. I noticed his discouragement seeping into the leaders gathered that evening. He complained about the lack of growth in front of those gathered. Later, as we drove to the airport, he doubted whether to stay at the church. I eventually blurted, "Who gives growth? You or God? You've done a great job and have an awesome church. Hang in there. God will give the growth in his timing."

Myth: If My Church Does Not Grow, I'm Not Successful

Pastors and leaders often feel like failures when they don't experience lots of growth. They expected all the cells to multiply in one year, which didn't happen. Few pastors are content where they are and desire more growth than they are experiencing at present.

Truth: Success Should be Measured by Faithful Effort Rather than Results

But the truth is that we are successful when we

faithfully serve Jesus! We can rejoice in the process of becoming like Jesus in our ministry.

Years ago, I was driven by numbers and felt like a ministry failure. Jesus began to show me my error of equating results with success in ministry. I realized that God considered me successful if I did my best to reach out and guide the cell vision according to his grace and wisdom. God showed me that he didn't want me to take responsibility for the fruit that only he could produce. After all, it is his church.

Years ago, I was doing a cell seminar with Mario Vega, the Elim Church lead pastor in San Salvador, El Salvador. Mario was talking about the rapid growth of Elim through evangelism and cell growth. During the break, a church planting team approached me. They were pioneering a church among an upper-class group in Guatemala. They wondered and doubted why they weren't experiencing the rapid growth Mario talked about. I encouraged them to pray and make their best effort to make disciples through the cell church strategy, knowing their target group was more resistant and challenging. I told them they were successful in the process of reaching out. After praying for them, I noticed tears streaming from their eyes. They needed freedom from the results-oriented condemnation that come from comparisons and expectations of church growth.

The same is true for you, pastor. Allow the Spirit of God to use you and guide you. He'll bring forth the fruit in his timing, and you'll be rewarded for your faithfulness.

Leadership Myths and Truths

Myth: It's Okay to Add Cell Ministry to What You Are Already Doing

Many pastors want to pile on cell ministry to what they are already doing. Perhaps they've heard about a thriving cell church and decided to add the model to their full schedule.

Truth: A Pastor Needs to Make Cell Ministry the Central Priority

As I studied cell churches worldwide, I kept hearing the phrase, "Cell Ministry is our backbone." Cell church is not simply an additional program but the church's base, much like an operating system on a computer. Other ministries flow from cell ministry, not the other way around.

When a church has fully transitioned to the cell strategy, everyone will be in a cell group before becoming involved in additional church ministries.

I tell pastors to count the cost before starting their cell church journey. It's better to fully prepare key leaders, start with a pilot group, and then grow into cell ministry rather than try to add cell church ministry as another program. Don't set yourself up for failure.

Myth: Lead Pastors Need to be Available to Everyone

Some pastors think they need to do everything. After, didn't they train to pastor the church? Aren't they getting paid?

Truth: Effective Cell Church Leaders Delegate

Ephesians 4 says that the leader's job is to prepare the laity to do the work of the ministry (Ephesians 4:11-12), not to do it themselves.

Wise cell church pastors understand that they must not be available to everyone. Rather they delegate. Before rushing to help church members, they will ask if the person has received help from their cell leader or team. Cell church pastors follow the proper chain of care and support and only take the more difficult cases like we read about in Exodus 18:17-18.

Myth: There Are Fewer Problems in the Cell Church than Traditional Ministry

People often want a quick fix, something to solve all their problems, so they think cell church ministry will give them fewer headaches and difficulties.

Truth: Cell Church Ministry Reveals Problems Often Hidden under the Busyness of Traditional Ministry

The reality is that cell church ministry helps people to express what's truly happening in their lives and gives them a chance to practice the advice of James, "Therefore confess your sins to each other and pray for each other so that you may be healed. The prayer of a righteous person is powerful and effective" (James 5:16).

As God's people start practicing transparency, it might appear that people have more problems, and the church is going downhill. Yet, in reality, the healing has just begun!

A doctor might diagnose a tumor and recommend removing it. The counsel is painful but wise patients follow it. Only after the operation can the healing begin.

During one seminar in Puerto Rico, a wise elder remarked that they didn't know the church had so many problems until they began cell group ministry. People were sharing their struggles and problems and church life seemed chaotic. However, over time, they experienced healing and blessings.

Traditional churches might look shiny, beautiful, and full of life. People sit, smile, and leave. Yet, they often are not dealing with struggles and problems that lurk below the surface.

Myth: If You Fail, Try Something Else

Truth: Failing Will Lead You to Discover What Works Best in Your Context

One of John Maxwell's books is *Failing Forward*. We learn the most through our mistakes. Someone said you must fail three times in cell ministry to get it right. I think you probably need to fail more.

Don't give up. Hang in there. Jesus is on your side, and he will use the process to mold you into a disciple-maker.

Reflection Questions

What did you learn from this lesson?

What was the myth/truth in this lesson that stood out to you?

Which myth/truth is God showing you to apply in your church?

Suggested Reading

Books

- Chapter 3-4 of *Myths and Truths of the Cell Church: Key Principles that Make or Break Cell Ministry*

Internet articles

Myth: If I Choose to Become a Cell Church, My Church Will Grow
Myth: Church Growth Is the Driving Motivation for Becoming a Cell Church
Myth: If My Church Does Not Grow, I'm Not Successful

Download this PowerPoint

Joel Comiskey's PowerPoint on this lesson:

https://tinyurl.com/mwvtaacz

CHAPTER 17

Myths and Truths: the Cell

WATCH THIS VIDEO ▶

https://youtu.be/-eeldg3X5Rs

C ell church ministry is not a legalistic strategy but a way to make better and more fruitful disciples. Sometimes, rather than making disciples through cell ministry, a well-intentioned pastor or leader can create and promote rules that weigh down the process. Rather than helping the flow of love and grace in the biblical discipleship process, cell ministry becomes legalistic and stagnant.

Cell focus myths and truths

Myth: All Groups Must be Homogeneous

One of those rules happened in a famous cell church in Latin America that dogmatically declared that all groups must work within the categories of men, women, children, or youth. No other homogeneity was permissible. Why? Some special anointing resided in these categories.

Truth: Allow Homogeneity to Naturally Develop as Cells Multiply

God uses a wide variety of homogeneity to make fruitful disciples. I advise starting with a quality definition and allowing homogeneity to flow naturally. For example, a holistic group will have *3-15 who meet weekly outside the church building for the purpose of evangelism, community, and spiritual growth with the goal of making disciples who make disciples that results in multiplication.*

Most cell churches highlight family cells. After all, the family is the base of the church and society. Other homogeneities, however, often flow naturally from family cells. New groups might reach specific homogeneity, such as men's cells, youth cells, and so forth.

Myth: One Person Should Be the Designated Host

Some churches have declared that the group cannot start unless there's a designated host or someone different from the leader. But where did they get this rule?

Truth: A Shared Hosting Arrangement Is Often the Best Option

I rejoice in those healthy cell churches with a separate host who has opened their house, but is this the only way to do it?

In the New Testament, the host of the house church was often also the leader.

Many cell churches rotate among the members to take turns hosting the cells. After all, when members step out, open their homes, and learn how to host, they will become more like Jesus as they learn to trust him.

And is it possible for the leader to also be the host? I've led groups with a variety of hosting options: groups from my home, those that rotated from house to house, and those that met in someone else's home. All hosting strategies have their place according to the needs and availability. Still, we must be careful not to add rules that might stagnate the process of making disciples who make disciples.

Myth: Asking Everyone to Be in a Cell Stifles the Use of Spiritual Gifts

Some churches position themselves as having a place for everyone's gifts and talents. "Come to my church and decide what you want to do and the ministry you want to create" is the philosophy of some churches. In an individualistic society, asking everyone to be in a cell group seems closed-minded.

Truth: The Cell Group is the Best Place to Discover Spiritual Gifts

The reality is that all New Testament gift passages were written to house churches. The small group environment is the best atmosphere for developing and allowing gift use. Of course, it's not the only place, but cell churches believe that each believer must initially grow in the small, intimate environment of the home cell group.

Those faithful in the little things will then be asked to use their gifts and talents in the larger church context.

Myth: The Cell Church Is All about the Cell

The cell is vital in the cell church movement, but is there more?

Truth: The Goal of the Cell Church Is to Make Disciples

Some don't believe me when I say, "I'm not a cell person." What? Yes, "I'm not primarily focused on the cell." I'm a discipleship person. It just so happens that the cell is the best atmosphere to form and shape future disciples.

Jesus chose this atmosphere when molding the twelve disciples. The early church met from house to house. Cell churches also highlight the equipping, coaching, and weekend celebrations, so the process is more than the cell. But we must never forget discipleship as the driving force.

Myth: Cells Are an Extension of the Sunday Service

Many pastors and churches employ small groups to close the back door. Any small group will do as long as they keep people returning to the Sunday services.

Truth: The Cell Is the Church

The reality is this: The cell is the church. The biblical writers use the word *ekklesia* to refer to the church in the house and the church of the city. *Ekklesia* is used for both. The writers of the New Testament didn't view those early house churches as incidental or add-ons. Nor should we.

For example, all of the Latin American cell churches in my initial study took offerings in the cell groups. They wanted to ensure that those attending participated in the entire church experience. Many cell groups celebrate the Lord's supper and baptize their people. Of course, everything is done in conjunction with the local church leadership.

Myth: Cells Should Encompass All Small Groups

It's easy to fall into the trap of making the small group definition very broad to accommodate all small groups. Often the motivation is to give people numerous options or to post more church growth statistics.

Truth: Start with a Quality Cell Definition

The reality is that if everything is a cell, nothing is a cell. A quality definition matters. Why? Discipleship. Strong disciples of Jesus have a far greater chance to grow and develop in a holistic small group than in a programmatic one. I'm not saying that spiritual growth doesn't occur in other ministries. I am saying that a holistic definition ensures quality control, which is essential in the disciple-making process.

Reflection Questions

What did you learn from this lesson?

What was the myth/truth in this lesson that stood out to you?

Which myth/truth is God showing you to apply in your church?

Suggested Reading

Books

- *Chapter 5-6 of Myths and Truths of the Cell Church. Key Principles that Make or Break Cell Ministry*

Internet articles

The Cell is the Church
Define Your Cell to Make Better Disciples
Why Cells Are the Best Place to Find and Develop Spiritual Gifts
Rotation Versus Permanent Hosting

Download this PowerPoint

Joel Comiskey's PowerPoint on this lesson:

https://tinyurl.com/2srzdjtn

CHAPTER 18

History of the Cell Church

WATCH THIS VIDEO ▶

https://youtu.be/vFrFYHZpZ50

The writer of Ecclesiastes had it right when he said, "There's nothing new under the sun." Even the most dynamic, growing cell churches today are versions of earlier models. Someone said, "If we don't learn from history, we will likely repeat it." Looking at small group movements throughout history, we can learn valuable principles to help us make mid-course corrections.

The biblical history of small groups goes back to approximately two million Israelites wandering in the desert with an overdependence on Moses to administer and take care of their needs. In Exodus 18, Jethro exhorted Moses to organize into groups of 10s, 50s, 100s, and 1000s. Moses obeyed Jethro's counsel and developed leaders for each level.

Years later, Jesus modeled small group ministry when he led a movement that met in homes throughout Galilee and Judea. He sent his disciples into homes to evangelize and multiply. When Pentecost happened in Acts Two, the disciples organized the multitude into house churches while preaching in the larger gatherings.

Paul repeatedly talked about preaching publicly and from house to house (Acts 20:20), and we know the early church was a house church movement. We must understand house-to-house ministry to understand the New Testament context.

When Constantine became emperor in 312 AD, everything changed. There was no longer a need for house-to-house ministry. Constantine employed many of the house church leaders to run the newly built cathedrals, and the world was plunged into the Dark Ages.

Many were disillusioned by the Constantinian church and rebelled by finding God in the desert and wilderness. Many felt the need to purify the church, and some decided to meet in groups for community. They were known as monks who met in monasteries. Often the monks tried to earn their salvation through good works, but other movements resembled those of the early church.

Saint Patrick's *Celtic movement* represented a return to New Testament Christianity. His method of ministry was to establish small groups of believers and invite the heathen to "taste and see" that the Lord is good. God used these communities to convert heathen tribes, and then Patrick prepared them to start new communities.

The *Brethren of the Common Life* was another home-grown movement within the Catholic Church. They met from house to house and multiplied when they reached twenty people. They wanted to be known as brothers rather than priests and lived in normal neighborhoods. Thomas O. Kempis came from this movement and wrote *The Imitation of Christ.*

Most of the small group movements found expression outside the Catholic hierarchy and experienced persecution because of their biblical beliefs.

God converted Peter Waldo in France and gave him a deep hunger for God's Word. He went everywhere preaching the gospel and even tried to get permission from Rome. When Waldo didn't answer all the questions precisely, the Catholic hierarchy wouldn't allow him to preach, but he continued to preach the gospel everywhere. Many were converted and met from house to house to love one another, study God's Word, and practice New Testament Christianity. Waldo's movement became known as the *Waldenses*.

John Wycliffe translated the Bible into English, and his followers were called the *Lollards*. They believed the Bible was the only authoritative guide and rejected Catholic tradition, including the pope's primacy, transubstantiation, and canon law. Many Lollards were burnt at the stake for their convictions.

John Hus, a disciple of Wycliff, brought Wycliff's teaching to Prague. Hus, a priest of a prominent church, preached from the pulpit the authority of God's Word. Many priests and bishops were converted, but soon, the Roman hierarchy resisted and set a trap for Hus. They deceived Hus and burned him at the stake. Yet, Hus's followers, aptly named the *Hussites*, continued to meet in small groups throughout Bohemia, studying God's Word, growing in their faith, and resisting Catholic dictates.

Luther, an Augustinian monk, agonized over trying to perfect himself through good works and rediscovered the biblical truth of justification by faith alone, through grace alone, and from the Bible alone. He also preached the priesthood of all believers. Luther succeeded through the protection of German authorities. Luther believed in small groups but feared the splintering of the Reformation.

The *Anabaptists* believed in the core teaching of the Reformation, but they wanted to take Luther's teaching to its logical conclusion and baptize believing adults through immersion. They felt true believers should meet separately to worship, resisting the state religion of the Lutherans and Calvinists. The reformers persecuted the Anabaptists, and many lost their lives. Anabaptists met from house to house to practice New Testament Christianity.

The *Puritans* in England were primarily Calvinists but believed they needed to reform the Anglican hierarchy. The queen and king resisted their efforts, and many Puritans (separatists) fled to America, where they established a city set on a hill, complete with religious freedom. Puritans met in *conventicles* to apply Scripture and practice the one-anothers of Scripture. In England, they were forbidden from meeting in home groups but decided it was more important to obey God than man.

One of my heroes is Felipe Spener, a Lutheran pastor in the 1700s who promoted spirituality among the clergy and his congregation. Spener is the father of modern evangelicalism because he taught the godly transformation of the Christian faith and not simply belief in certain theological truths. He wrote a famous book, *Pia Desideira* (Godly Living), in which he talked about personal devotions, meeting in small groups, and personal godliness. Spener transformed his sermon notes into small group lessons and prepared the laity to lead church sponsored home groups. Before his death, he established a university called Halle, which continued teaching pietistic principles.

Count Zinzendorf, a student at Halle, became a disciple of Spener's pietistic teaching. He was also wealthy and owned large swathes of land. He invited the Hussites to live on his land and guided them to meet in small groups called bands. The unique aspect of Zinzendorf's pietistic vision was his emphasis on small-group evangelism. He sent these bands worldwide, and God gave birth to the modern *Moravian* missionary movement.

God used the Moravians to convert John Wesley. Wesley visited Zinzendorf's bands and took notes. Welsey started a similar small group movement in England with specific adaptations. Wesley believed that preaching without establishing small groups was fruitless. By his death, he left 10,000 small groups and 100,000 in the larger celebrations. A member attending the larger gatherings had to show proof of attendance in the small groups. Wesley's movement became known as the *Methodist* movement.

The modern-day small group movement continues the waves of small group revivals that we see in church history, emphasizing similar characteristics. Many believe David Cho is the father of the modern day cell movement, growing his church to 25,000 cells and 250,000 people.

Worldwide mega cell churches abound, but so do church-planting movements. The cell is the church, and those small groups gather to worship together and hear God's Word.

I detail these movements in my book *2000 Years of Small Groups*. Pastor, God desires to guide and bless you as you establish small groups in your church.

Reflection Questions

What did you learn from this lesson?

What historical small group movement impresses you the most? Why?

How can you apply the lessons from these movements to your own small group ministry?

Suggested Reading

Books

- Chapters 1-15 of *2000 Years of Small Groups: A History of Cell Ministry in the Church*

Internet articles

The Demise of the House Church
Small Groups and Monasticism
Small Groups During the Pre-Reformation
Luther and Small Groups
Wesley and Small Groups
History of the Modern-day Cell Movement

Download this PowerPoint

Joel Comiskey's PowerPoint on this lesson:

https://tinyurl.com/nwjkcmf8

CHAPTER 19

Children in Cell Ministry

WATCH THIS VIDEO ▶

https://youtu.be/CGSxeL6SK9g

My journey with children in cell ministry began in Ecuador when we asked our Christian Education director to prepare cell lessons for our children's cell groups. And then, in Moreno Valley, California, we started a church from my home, and my young daughters led the children's cell group.

However, I only grasped the power of children's cell groups when I wrote the book *Children in Cell Ministry*. The book opened my eyes to what God is doing worldwide to make disciples through children.

The Bible is the first place to start. Jesus would often stop everything he was doing to minister to the children. He told us that we needed to become like little children to enter the Kingdom of God and that the greatest in the Kingdom were children. We know the early house churches thrived with children, many of them orphans. Were they with the adults all the time? In separate rooms? We're not 100% sure. The Old Testament is also chocked full of exhortations to teach children the ways of God at all times.

I also learned about the early pioneers of children's small group ministry. Ralph Neighbour, for example, back in the 1980s noticed adults trying to teach the children on those giant steps of Yoido Full Gospel Church in South Korea, and believed there was a better way. He returned to Houston to perfect intergenerational cell groups in which the adults and children interacted together. Daphne Kirk and Lorna Jenkins were also early pioneers in implementing children's cell ministry.

I noticed that pastors who have thriving children's ministries envision the future now. They don't wait for youth ministry but take seriously the need to disciple children. I think of pastor Keison in Barquisimeto, Venezuela. He visited Wales to learn about the past revivals and their history. He was disappointed to discover huge, empty buildings. God spoke to him, saying, "Unless you prioritize the children now, you'll end up the same." He went back to Barquisimeto and prioritized children. When I was with him, I noticed beautiful Sunday school rooms and 250 cell groups for children.

Then there's the Vine Church in Goiania, Brazil. They have 10,000 children's cell groups worldwide, with some 2000 children's cells in the mother church. They are committed to disciple children in the same way they disciple adults.

The goal of the cell church is to make disciples who make disciples. But does this apply primarily to adults? No. We need to also see children as disciples who must grow and develop.

Cell church is a two-winged ministry. That is, disciples are formed and shaped in cell and celebration—not one or the other. Most of us know or have experienced children's Sunday school and training for children on Sunday. Teaching children on Sunday is excellent since most conversions occur before age fourteen.

Cell churches take training one step further and apply the Sunday teaching to the cell groups. But what type of children's cell groups?

In children's cell ministry today, there are two main types of cell groups. One is called intergenerational cell groups, and the other is what I call *children-only cell groups*.

Intergenerational groups mix adults with children. The early church most likely featured intergenerational cell groups. Parents normally bring their children, but children might invite their friends. The beauty of IG groups is connecting the generations together. The older adults feel younger with children present, and children benefit from the wisdom aging brings.

Many IG groups will make an agreement between parents about their children's behavior. The agreement might include *no running in the house, no writing on walls, jumping on furniture, etc.*

Normally in IG groups the kids meet with the adults for the icebreaker and worship. Leaders must be sensitive to including the children as much as possible. Then, the children go into another room for the lesson time. Two adults or youth should lead the lesson time. If no adult is specifically called to lead the children's cell, the members can rotate among themselves with the hope that someone will feel called to become the children's cell leader.

During the refreshment time, the children will often present what they learned to the adults in a drama or story form.

Many churches around the world are effectively implementing IG groups with much fruit.

The other type of cell group is called children-only cells, or CO groups. In these groups, the focus is on the children from beginning to end. CO groups might take place in the backyard or in another room of the house. Often, they happen after school in a specific neighborhood.

The Elim Church puts a lot of effort and training into CO groups. Jenny, for example, went through more than one year of training to prepare to be a children's cell leader at the Elim Church. She started leading a children's cell in a poor neighborhood of San Salvador. Leonel was one of the children who started coming to the CO group. He lived with his grandmother because his mother could not care for him. Gangs and evil influences were everywhere, but Jenny paid particular attention to Leonel, helping him memorize Scripture and participate in the cell group. Leonel escaped the enemy's snare by God's grace and continued following Jesus. When I interviewed both Jenny and Leonel, I rejoiced that Leonel was enrolled in the university and a vibrant part of the Elim youth ministry.

The Vine church is an excellent example of CO groups. The Vine planted a church in Cusco, Perú that grew exponentially. Why? CO groups. I heard that Cusco was a graveyard for evangelical churches, and it's true that most struggle. The Vine is different. José Luis picked me up from the airport, shared his conversion in a children's cell group, and how he became a youth cell leader. He was then serving on the pastoral team. The majority of the eleven pastors at the Vine Church were converted as children in children's cells. At the time of my visit, the Cusco Vine Church had 900 cell groups, and 450 were children's cell groups.

Churches that reap the harvest with children's cell groups pay careful attention to equipping the entire church, starting with the children. Some cell churches have entire equipping tracks geared toward children. All prioritize training children by ensuring that the equipping is intertwined with lots of stories and drama. Children love to act out what they learned and learn best when they experience teaching. Churches often fail when they overlook the spirituality of children and don't trust that the children can hear from God, pray for others, and use their gifts.

One reason for failure is not equipping the parents. Parents must bring their children to cell groups, open their houses, and participate in leadership. Even though the church in Barquisimeto, Venezuela had 250 children's cell groups, the leaders confessed that the most significant problem was the lack of parental involvement. Parents can so easily forget that they were children at one time. Some parents have to overcome their unbelief and remember that God starts with children when making disciples who make disciples.

Churches that prioritize children and reap the harvest take the discipleship of children seriously. They are also very protective of children and make sure that all children's cell groups are led by two leaders who have been fully approved by the church leadership and have a clean record with the local authorities. One fundamental rule is that a adult should *never be alone with a child*. Child abuse is very real, and Christ's church needs to walk in purity and uprightness before the Lord and local authorities.

Above all, pray. Making disciples of children is a spiritual battle, and we need to start by winning the war through prayer.

Reflection Questions

What did you learn from this lesson?

What do you need to do to prioritize children in cell ministry?

If you do not have children's cell group, what will you do to start the process?

How will you avoid the dangers and failures of children in cell ministry mentioned in this lesson?

Suggested Reading

Books

- *Chapters 1-11 of Children in Cell Ministry: Discipling the Future Generation Now*

Internet articles

The Biblical Base for Children in Cell Ministry
Discipling Children through the Cell System
Intergenerational Cell Groups
Children Only Cell Groups
Equipping the Children
Mistakes in Children's Ministry

Download this PowerPoint

Joel Comiskey's PowerPoint on this lesson:

https://tinyurl.com/yw38rmtt

CHAPTER 20

Youth in Cell Ministry

WATCH THIS VIDEO ▶

https://youtu.be/fzN5VGuuivo

My Journey

My journey into small group ministry started when I was nineteen years old. God showed me I would be leading a Bible study. Not long afterward, my younger brother, Andy, approached me to help some younger believers grow in their faith. We met weekly at my parents' house, rotating between their house and the next-door neighbor's. I was only two years old in Jesus but grew as I dished out my limited knowledge to others.

One evening, a missionary spoke in our home group, and God called me to become a missionary. Those days were filled with excitement because it was the tail end of the Jesus movement in southern California, and God was moving powerfully.

God has always worked through young people. Here's a cursory example of God's movement among youth:

Biblical Background for Youth Ministry

Joseph was a "young man of seventeen years" when God interrupted him while he was sleeping with incredible dreams (Genesis 37:5). God eventually used Joseph to save the world from famine and deliver his family.

- Joshua was Moses' helper from "his youth" (Numbers 11:28) and guided the Israelites into the promised land.
- Samuel is another excellent example of God's call to young people. He first heard God's voice and call as a child. When Samuel was "old and gray," he testified that from his

youth, he had been a leader for the people of Israel (1 Samuel 12:2).

- Ruth was still a young woman when she was widowed and followed Naomi to Bethlehem (Ruth 1).
- David was a mere boy when he defeated Goliath and attracted the king's attention. David's character development and feats of faith began when he was a shepherd boy, tending sheep (1 Samuel 17).
- Daniel and his friends were probably teenagers, and they testified for Yahweh and interpreted the king's dreams (Daniel 1-5).
- Mary, the mother of Jesus, was a young girl when the angel appeared to her with unprecedented news of her supernatural pregnancy (Luke 1:26-38).
- Some consider Jesus to have led the first "youth group," and it is believed that Christ's twelve disciples were probably under eighteen.
- The apostle Paul began working with Timothy when he was approximately sixteen. Paul discipled Timothy and prepared him to become pastor of Ephesus, a significant church. He exhorted his young disciple: "Let no one despise you for being young. On the contrary,

let the believers see in you an example to follow in the way you speak, in your conduct,
and in love, faith and purity" (1 Timothy 4:12).

Window of Opportunity

We must remember that the majority of people are
converted before 18 years of age (and most before
14). We must take advantage of this window of
opportunity to reach them. God used Luis Bush to
promote and prioritize the 10/40 window, the geo-
graphical area where most of the unreached peoples
of the world live. Later, Luis Bush focused his attention on the 4/14 window, which refers to the ages of
four to fourteen in which most people receive Jesus
as Lord and Savior.

Relational Discipleship

Techniques for reaching youth abound. Some believe
concerts, game nights, and food parties are the best
ways to reach young people today.

While we must experiment with what works best
in particular contexts, relational outreach is biblical
and meaningful for youth today. Young people are
looking for family ties and a sense of belonging. Peer

influence is strong, and we must offer them God's love through community.

Carlos grew up in a broken home in San Salvador. He had never heard his mother tell him she loved him, and his father had left the home when he was young. Carlos descended into the world of drugs. By God's grace, he accepted the invitation to attend an Elim cell group where he heard the gospel of Jesus Christ. The leader approached Carlos after the cell, saying, "Jesus knows your sadness and wants to help you."

Carlos collapsed in tears, received Jesus, and found a new family.

He never returned to drugs after that day. Jesus filled his heart, and he became part of a new family. He went back to his parents and asked for forgiveness. Carlos continued growing as Christ's disciple, eventually leading a cell group.

Jesus desires to reach people in an atmosphere of love and care. He has come to extend to people a new family, the family of God.

Organic Youth System

Small group ministry offers an organic way to do ministry rather than a programmatic formula. God uses the cell church to reach youth in the cell, congregation, and the celebration.

The definition of a youth cell group is the same as that of adults: 3-15 people who meet weekly outside the church building for the purpose of evangelism, community, and spiritual growth. The goal is to make disciples who make disciples, which results in multiplication.

Effective cell groups meet weekly to maintain the discipleship edge. They also penetrate a lost world by meeting outside the church building. The church building is wonderful for training, coaching, and Sunday celebrations, but cell groups meet where non-Christians live and work.

Most youth cells will meet in homes, but some might meet in a Starbucks, park, university campus, or other unique venues. The goal is to make disciples who make other disciples.

Youth also need to congregate. I'm referring to youth cell groups coming together for a distinct gathering or activity. How often? While it can be weekly, some youth ministries meet once per month.

Like all church members, youth are also encouraged to attend the weekly celebration gatherings, where God's Word is preached and members worship together. Cells, congregations, and celebrations are the primary ways youth gather. What do youth cells look like? I noticed two types of youth cells. The first is the intergenerational youth cell.

Intergenerational Youth Cells

An intergenerational youth cell group follows the typical definition of a cell. The order is also similar—welcome, worship, word, and witness.

The main difference is that youth meet with adults in a mixed-cell group, and children might also be present.

iRest in Reseda, California, has some 500 cell groups. At iRest, the youth are mixed in with the adults. They feel it is a powerful way for youth to connect with the generations. The youth have congregational meetings and plan events separately but in the cell groups, they mix with all generations.

Brian Kannel, lead pastor of York Alliance Church in York, PA, also promotes his church's intergenerational youth cell groups. He touts the encouragement youth receive when they go to university and the new life they breathe into the older generation. Pastor Brian admitted that it is harder for youth to invite non-Christian friends to an intergenerational cell group.

Evangelism is one reason why youth cells often decide to launch youth-led cell groups.

Youth-Led Cell Groups

Dove Christian Fellowship started with intergenerational youth cell groups but discovered that the youth had a yearning to start their own cell groups. Dove still has both types, but youth-led cell groups have given them more evangelistic outreach and a more in-depth discipleship edge.

The Elim Church in San Salvador has a similar story. During its early history, it only promoted mixed cell groups with youth and adults attending the same group. Yet, it also noticed the same yearning for youth to start their own groups. Today, Elim has hundreds of youth-led cell groups within each of its districts.

Equipping and Coaching

All cell churches primarily promote making disciples who make other disciples. They do so through cell, celebration, equipping, and coaching.

The same is true in youth cell ministry. For cell groups to flourish among youth, it is essential to train and coach future youth leaders. Youth need both equipping and coaching to succeed.

Mistakes in Youth Cell Ministry

One error in youth ministry is the need for more consistency. Many youth pastors and leaders view youth ministry as a stepping stone to adult ministry, rather than a specific calling. Fruitful youth ministry flourishes with leaders who are willing to minister long-term.

Another error is not preparing the parents. Youth do not have their own homes and might also need transportation. Parents must fill the gap, opening their homes and hearts for youth.

Another area for improvement is to take the work of prayer seriously when preparing the youth. We must remember the spiritual battle and God's love for young people.

Reflection Questions

What did you learn from this lesson?

What are you doing to reach the youth through cell ministry? How can you improve?

How will you avoid the mistakes of youth ministry as mentioned in this chapter?

Suggested Reading

Books

- Chapters1-13: *Youth in Cell Ministry: Discipling the Next Generation Now*

Internet articles

Biblical Base for God Using Youth
Understanding Youth Today
Intergenerational Youth Cells
Youth-led Cells

Download this PowerPoint

Joel Comiskey's PowerPoint on this lesson:

https://tinyurl.com/5e7zn6yr

CHAPTER 21

Living in Victory

WATCH THIS VIDEO ▶

https://youtu.be/kLWO0eKy0Xk

God wants us to live in victory. He has created us for himself and equipped us to bear fruit and live abundant lives. But how do we do this? I want to offer some principles that I believe will make a difference in your life and ministry.

#1 Keep the End In View

God tells us that the best is yet to come. Revelation 21:4 says, "He will wipe every tear from their eyes. There will be no more death' or mourning or crying or pain, for the old order of things has passed away." We will face problems in this life, but it helps immensely to know that something far better awaits us. The Bible tells us to set our affections on things above and not on things of this earth. We live in victory as we get our eyes off ourselves and on our creator.

#2 Experience God's Love

Only as we experience God's love can we truly love others. John tells us that God is love. He says, "And so we know and rely on the love God has for us. God is love. Whoever lives in love lives in God, and God in them" (1 John 4:16). Jude tells us to keep ourselves in his love. His love is rock solid, and nothing can separate us from his perfect love. Maybe your parents were not there for you, but please don't project their love on God. His love is deep, rich, and continual.

#3 Receive God's Grace

The Bible tells us that the Christian life starts and finishes with his grace. His grace justifies us and makes us righteous because of what Jesus has done for us on the cross. But grace also works in us to make us more like Jesus. The Bible calls this process sanctification. Paul says, "But by the grace of God I am what I am, and his grace to me was not without effect. No, I worked harder than all of them—yet not I, but the grace of God that was with me" (1 Corinthians 15:10). God's grace frees us to live a victorious Christian life.

#4 Trust That God Is In Control

When we believe that God controls all things, we can walk confidently, knowing and believing what Paul says in Romans 8:28: "And we know that in all things God works for the good of those who love him, who have been called according to his purpose." Nothing can happen outside God's plan, and he is in control of all things. We can live victoriously when we realize that no evil can touch us part from God's all-pervasive plan and will.

#5 Spend Daily Time With God

Yesterday's blessing won't suffice for today. Each day has enough trouble, and we need daily spiritual food. Jesus told us to pray, "Give us today our daily bread" (Matthew 6:11). We need both physical and spiritual food daily. Taking time for daily devotions is essential to the Christian life. Some pastors only spend time alone with God when preparing their sermons, but feeding our souls in God's Word, prayer, and worship is necessary.

#6 Invest in Your Intimate Circle

Ephesians 5 to 6 discuss the importance of our inner circle, explicitly prioritizing our families. True success is having those closest to us love and respect us the most. They know who we are up close, and living the Christian life before them is essential. They are our priority. We can be successful with those who don't know us, but it's also easy to project an image that doesn't align with reality.

#7 Get Connected with God's Family

I'm referring here to the local church. You might say, "But I'm a pastor. Of course, I'm connected to the local church." But notice what Luke says in Acts: "They devoted themselves to the apostles' teaching and to fellowship, to the breaking of bread and to prayer. . . Every day they continued to meet together in the temple courts. They broke bread in their homes and ate together with glad and sincere hearts" (Acts 2:42,46). Luke is talking here about a two-winged church. Are you connected to a small group where you can receive from and give to others?

#8 Make Time for Rest

God has created us to work six days per week and rest one day. God did not create us to work 24/7. We need rest. The particular day is not as important as separating one day off to rest. From the beginning, God said, "Remember the Sabbath day by keeping it holy. Six days you shall labor and do all your work, but the seventh day . . .you shall not do any work, . . For in six days the LORD made the heavens and the earth, the sea, and all that is in them, but he rested on the seventh day" (Exodus 20:8-11). Are you taking one full day to rest?

#9 Care for Your Body

The first principle was to start with eternity in mind. We will soon be with Jesus. Yet, while in this body, we must take care of it. Notice how Paul describes our bodies, "Do you not know that your bodies are members of Christ himself?. . Do you not know that your bodies are temples of the Holy Spirit, who is in you, whom you have received from God? You are not your own; you were bought at a price. Therefore honor God with your bodies" (1 Corinthians 6:15–20). Our bodies are God's temple. He lives in them. We need to care for them as his vessels.

I've expounded these principles in my book *Living in Victory: 9 Spiritual Truths for Transformation and Renewal.* I pray that Jesus fills you and uses you for his glory.

Reflection Questions

What did you learn from this lesson?

Of the nine principles Comiskey mentioned, which one stood out to you? How will you allow Jesus to implement that principle?

How can you apply these principles to your daily life?

Suggested Reading

Books

- *Chapters 1-10 of Living in Victory: 9 Spiritual Truths for Transformation and Renewal*

Internet articles

Trust in God's Providence
God's Grace Works in Us
Asking God to Work in the Dark Areas
Daily Soul Care
Prioritizing Your Intimate Circle
Taking One Day Off
The Need for Exercise

Download this PowerPoint

Joel Comiskey's PowerPoint on this lesson:

https://tinyurl.com/3m77vfsy

www.ingramcontent.com/pod-product-compliance
Lightning Source LLC
LaVergne TN
LVHW051408080426
835508LV00022B/2991

* 9 7 8 1 9 5 0 0 6 9 6 1 3 *